PRESENCES OF JESUS

Presences of Jesus

Carl J. Pfeifer

TWENTY-THIRD PUBLICATIONS
Mystic, Connecticut

© 1984 by Carl J. Pfeifer. No part of this book should be
reproduced by any means without permission of the publisher.
For such permission address:
Permissions Editor, Twenty-Third Publications,
P.O. Box 180, Mystic, CT 06355

Edited by Marie McIntyre and John G. van Bemmel
Designed by John G. van Bemmel
Cover by Robert Maitland
ISBN 0-89622-211-X
Library of Congress Catalog Card No. 84-50163

DEDICATION

To the Jesuits,
   the Society of Jesus,
who taught me
   to find Christ
      present
         in all of life.

Contents

Introduction

*I*t was an interesting evening. We were talking about Jesus Christ. But we were surprised at what we heard ourselves saying. "That's what I believe this evening," Joan admitted, "but I wouldn't have said that ten years ago."

We had gathered, about fifteen of us, to share what Jesus meant to us. We wanted to deepen our knowledge of him. We hoped to explore the Church's teachings about Jesus.

To stimulate our thoughts and feelings, we looked at a series of pictures of Jesus. They were the work of artists from the time of the catacombs to our contemporary world. We compared the artists' images with our own personal images of Jesus. We found that we each had, like the various artists, a slightly different picture of Jesus in our imaginations. The variety of images encouraged questioning.

Our initial questions were about what Jesus was *really* like. What did he look like? Did he know who he was? Did he know everything or did he learn from experience? Did he make mistakes? Did Jesus ever fall in love? Was he a liberal? a revolutionary? Did he experience real temptations, as we do? Did he really suffer? Did Jesus know he would rise from the dead? What did he expect to accomplish?

From these intriguing questions about Jesus' personality and experience, we moved to another set of questions. What difference does Jesus Christ make today? Where can we meet him today? When? How? What can it possibly mean to call this man "God"? How is Jesus Christ unique?

Our questions surprised us a bit. Some of our answers

9

were even more unexpected. We noticed how our questions centered around a curiosity about what Jesus was like as a human being, and around his continued importance.

Our responses to the first set of questions—as well as the questions themselves—betrayed a lurking doubt about Jesus' humanness. We seemed to fear some of the answers we were now giving to questions which we would have answered quite differently as little as ten years ago. What was clear was that we accepted the Catholic teaching about Jesus being "true man" as well as "true God," but felt more comfortable with that doctrine as long as it remained in the abstract. When we touched down on Jesus' possible thoughts, feelings, questions, temptations, anxieties, doubts, we became less sure of ourselves.

The questions about Jesus' uniqueness and continuing importance revealed a deep desire to relate more meaningfully with him now, in today's world. We seemed to be looking to Christ Jesus as a source of assurance that we were basically sound and that the world was ultimately for us, rather than against us.

At every point of our questioning we seemed to meet a common frustration. The language with which we were familiar from our earlier religious education was not completely helpful. The catechism, and even the creeds, seemed to be very abstract. Their language did not speak very well to us in response to the kinds of human questions of meaning that concerned us. Creed language did not seem to move or inspire us.

We ended this illuminating evening, the first of several, with a brief prayer experience. As we looked again at slides of sacred art portraying Jesus, we listened to the melody of "Day by Day," the ancient prayer popularized in the rock musical, *Godspell*. With our eyes contemplating the faces of Christ, our hearts prayed quietly "to see thee more clearly, to love thee more dearly, to follow thee more nearly, day by day." It was a beautiful experience. We sensed the presence of Jesus.

The course of our group sharing and prayer that evening reflect some of the major trends in the theological approach to Jesus Christ in recent years. The study of Christ, or "christology," has developed dramatically in the Church over the past decade. Major theologians in all parts of the world have turned their attention to reinterpreting the traditional faith of Christians in Jesus Christ. There has been a renewed search for the "historical Jesus"—what Jesus was really like as he lived, preached, and worked remarkable deeds in Galilee and Judaea. Somehow, the theologians seem to find in the "Jesus of history" significant clues about the "Christ of faith." In the process much of what most of us learned from the catechism has been turned upside down—and found still to be true!

The catechism might be said to begin "from above," from the perspective of God. The starting point is that Jesus Christ is God, the second person of the Blessed Trinity, who became man. The questions posed from this starting point are mainly two: *How can God become man?* and *How can Jesus be both God and man at the same time?*

The catechism answers indicate that God became human through the incarnation. God the Son took to himself a human nature like ours. This was accomplished through the power of the Holy Spirit and the willing cooperation of the Virgin Mary, without any human father intervening. Jesus was both God and a man because he was but one divine person having two natures, one divine and one human. As "God made human beings," Jesus Christ is "Savior of all human beings."

Such, in summary, is the teaching of the Baltimore Catechism. It is a teaching with a very long history in the Church, going back in almost identical words to the fourth century. The faith expressed in the language of the catechism goes back, of course, to the apostles and the first Christian communities. But the particular way of expressing that faith—for example, the language of the Baltimore Catechism—took shape during the exciting ecumenical councils of the Church in the fourth and fifth centuries: Nicea (325), Ephesus (431), and Chalcedon (451).

The Nicene Creed, which we pray together at Mass each Sunday, preserves the classical formulation of the Church's understanding of Jesus Christ. It arose through the intense controversies that led up to these important Church councils. The language of the Creed is the same as that of the catechism. That language has been preserved unchanged for three-fourths of the Church's history. Millions of Christians have prayed through the centuries: "We believe . . . in one Lord, Jesus Christ, the only Son of God, eternally begotten of the Father, God from God, Light from Light, true God from true God, begotten, not made, one in Being with the Father. Through Him all things were made. For us and for our salvation, he came down from heaven: and became man . . . ."

The classical approach to christology begins "from above," from God, and struggles with how God can become a man and how God and people can be one in Jesus Christ. It deals with these questions because, at that time, these were the questions being asked, and argued.

An influential priest named Arius claimed Jesus could only be God's adopted son. According to Arius, Jesus was a great man, perhaps the greatest of all human beings, but he could not be called God. An important bishop, Nestorius, also taught that Jesus, as Mary's son, was just a man, but a man in whom God's Word dwelt as in a temple.

On the other side of the argument were those who insisted that Jesus was God, but was not really human. A wealthy shipowner, Marcion, whose father was a bishop, taught people that Jesus was God appearing in human form. Bishop Apollinaris partially agreed with Marcion. He believed Jesus was God, that he had a human body, but that God took the place of Jesus' soul. An abbot of a large monastery, a monk named Eutyches preached that God's son fused into a unity with himself the son of Mary. In fact, then, Jesus was not really human.

So for two centuries the battle raged. Popes became involved. Emperors convoked councils. Finally, on October 31, 451, in the basilica of Saint Euphonia in Chalcedon, 350 bishops agreed with the statement read by one of the legates from Pope Leo. "We all in one accord teach the profession of faith in the one identical Son, our Lord Jesus Christ. We declare that he is perfect both in his divinity and in his humanity, truly God and truly man composed of body and rational soul; that he is consubstantial with the Father in his divinity, consubstantial with us in his humanity, like us in every respect except for sin."

Fifty years later, a learned man, Gelasius, summed up in similar words the classical teaching about Jesus. "The Lord Jesus Christ is one and the same person. The whole God is man, and the whole man is God. Whatever there is of humanity, the God-man makes his own. Whatever there is of God, the man-God possesses. The whole man continues to be what God is, and the whole God continues to be whatever man is. This remains a profound mystery."

There is a noble simplicity, an eloquent wholeness, to these ancient formulations of what the Church of the time believed about Jesus Christ. The very simplicity, nobility, eloquence, and solidity of the classical christological creed has made it the touchstone of orthodox faith in Jesus Christ ever since. The Church will continue to reaffirm our cherished faith in Jesus Christ with these ancient creeds. They remain a priceless treasure of authentic Christian beliefs.

But theologians—and many of the faithful at large— find that these formulations from an ancient world seem less adequate today in helping people understand Jesus Christ and express their commitment to him. Part of the reason is that we are asking somewhat different questions from those that the Christians of the 4th and 5th centuries were asking. A comparison of our study group's questions and those that led to the Councils of Nicea, Ephesus, and Chalcedon reveals the difference. We are asking about Jesus from a search for meaning and identity in a world filled with anxiety, alienation, and nuclear bombs. We want to know about Jesus— much as we search in ourselves—how he felt about himself, how he coped with life, what gave him a sense of meaning and purpose, how he handled difficulties, what made him happy, how he found fulfillment.

These are not the questions addressed by the creeds and catechisms. The 350 bishops gathered at Chalcedon in 451 were not troubled by such questions. Our questions arise in a world that seems to be coming apart, that seems to be getting beyond our control. Our language is shaped by science and technology, history and evolution, psychotherapeutic theory and practice. Our media are television, movies, novels, and computer printouts.

Their world was embraced by the mighty Empire, whose center was shifting from Rome to Constantinople (modern Istanbul). Their language was shaped by Greek philosophy, art, theater. That worldview and language looked at order, beauty, truth, ideal forms, and changeless essences. Its media were the writings of Greek philosophers, dramatists, and poets.

It is not surprising, then, that their answers fail to respond adequately to our questions. Where we search to discover what Jesus was really like, they describe Jesus' metaphysical makeup. While we grapple with Jesus' experiences, thoughts, and feelings, they tell us of his "person" and "nature." In their language we may not even call Jesus a human person, yet in our language not to call Jesus a human person means he is not fully human. In fact, what they mean by "person" and "nature" is not what we mean today by the very same words.

So theologians are struggling to put into modern terms the same faith in Jesus Christ that the ancient creeds expressed so well to the people of their own times. Contemporary theologians realize that the approach and language of classical christology differs considerably from our own. We approach Jesus Christ from a quite different perspective and seek to explain him in quite different language.

Curiously, another motive for reinterpreting the ancient creeds is that they are as different from the world of the New Testament as they are from our twentieth-century world. Peter, Paul, and even John would be just as uncomfortable with "nature," person," and "consubstantial," as we are. They would be even less inclined perhaps than we are to try to understand Jesus Christ "from above," starting from God rather than from human experience. There are notable differences between the New Testament attempts to explain Jesus Christ and those of classical christology.

For example, the central experience of Christ in the New Testament—the one experience that most reveals who Jesus is and what he does—is the resurrection. The New Testament begins, as it were, with Easter which, of course, includes the death of Jesus as well as his resurrection. It is the Cross that unlocks the mystery of Jesus' life and importance. The experience of the risen Lord three days after he was killed is the central moment of insight into Jesus Christ.

Yet in the classical christology preserved in the creeds and catechism, the central event is the incarnation of God as man. The nativity becomes central, with Jesus' death merely completing his incarnation and the resurrection confirming Jesus' divinity. Christmas seems more important than Easter.

Another striking difference between Gospels and creed or catechism touches on Jesus' ministry. Starting from the resurrection experience, the disciples of Jesus looked back to the words and deeds of Jesus during his ministry. There they found hints of his real identity and mission, the full discovery of which they realized only in Jesus' resurrection from death. The bulk of the Gospel narrative reveals Jesus as Lord and Christ through his words and actions described by the disciples in the light of the resurrection experience. In the Gospel stories "who Jesus is" is seen through "what he does." His identity is intimately linked with his mission, his work. By contrast, classical christology omits altogether the ministry of Jesus. The creeds and the catechism jump from Jesus' birth to his passion and death: ". . . and became man. For our sake he was crucified. . . ." The essential identity of Jesus and his fundamental mission are reasoned to abstractly, beginning from the incarnation. Who Jesus is and what he does are not closely intertwined as in the Gospels. While creed and catechism carefully point out that God became man "for us and for our salvation," they do not spell out that saving work in relation to the personality of Jesus as revealed in his ministry. As a result, many a believer has felt, in reading the Gospels in the light of the creed and catechism, that Jesus was playing out a prewritten script chiefly for our edification and example.

Since the customary approach to Jesus found in the creeds and catechism does not readily speak the language of the Gospels nor of our contemporary world, recent studies of Christ take as their points of departure the New Testament and contemporary human experience. From these two poles, they attempt to reinterpret the classical approaches to Christ in order to preserve the traditional faith of the creed and catechism but in more experiential and biblical language.

Beginning from human experience, theologians today make rich use of the human sciences. Some, like Karl Rahner and Hans Küng, search into human aspirations with the help of anthropology. Teilhard de Chardin preferred to probe the evolutionary processes of the cosmos. Third World liberation theologians delve into the movements of peoples struggling against oppression. From whichever starting point—human nature, cosmos, history—the search leads to the same questions: *What difference (to humanity, the world, its history) does Jesus Christ make? What makes him so special among all men and women? What was he really like?*

To respond to those questions, contemporary theologians turn directly to the Gospels. They seek to discover all they can about Jesus of Nazareth. Probing through layers of tradition that make up the Gospels, they hope to catch a glimpse of Jesus of Nazareth as his contemporaries may have seen him in Capernaum or Jerusalem. Such a search requires the most sophisticated tools of modern scientific biblical research. Despite the layers of tradition that at once cloak and reveal the historical features of Jesus, scholars today feel quite confident that they are able to discover not only some of Jesus' actual words and deeds, but the general attitudes that governed his life and his self-awareness.

The man whose main personality traits are still discernible through the layers of interpretation that make up the Gospels is fascinating. His stunning claims to authority are translated into action in a life of humble service. Speaking for God, he seems most at home with sinners. Acting with awesome power, he raises not a finger to defend himself. He breaks God's laws to draw people to the heart of God's law. He speaks of life's profoundest mysteries in the simplest of stories. He does nothing but good—healing, forgiving, teaching, encouraging—but is condemned as a criminal. Close to God, whom he calls his Father, he is perceived as a threat to religion. He claims to die so others might live.

The fascinating portrait of Jesus of Nazareth that emerges from the stories of Jesus' ministry gives hints of his specialness, his unique importance, his divinity. His authentic words, actions, and inner attitudes suggest that he himself was aware of who he was and what his life would mean for the world. Theologians speak of these hints as an "implicit christology." What remained implicit during Jesus' lifetime became explicit only in the light of his death and resurrection. The Gospels, as we have them today, clearly articulate an "explicit christology" in which Jesus is acknowledged as "Lord" and "Savior," as "Son of God" while being "Mary's son." The divinity of Jesus and his saving mission is discovered through his life and ministry, his death and resurrection.

Modern approaches to the study of Christ generally follow this movement "from below"—from human experience and the Gospel portrait of Jesus. It is a movement advocated long ago by St. Augustine who wrote that "through the man Christ you move to the God Christ" (Sermon 261, 7).

This book is an attempt to present some of the findings of contemporary christology in a way that reveals something of this approach through the human to the divine. Much data will be explored from the Gospels. We will try to discover something of what Jesus of Nazareth was "really" like, and what we believe him to be for us today.

As our study group asked that evening, we want to deal with the questions of *who Jesus is* and *what difference he makes.* The answer to both questions brings us to the realization of his presence with us: "I am with you always" (Matthew 28:20). Our book is basically about the *presences of Jesus* and how we may come into contact with the living Christ, who is in fact the historical Jesus of Nazareth.

Each chapter follows an invariable progression, exemplifying the contemporary christology "from below," and culminating in a spirituality of Christ present:

A. Human experience—our needs and desires
B. Jesus of history—as revealed in Gospels
C. The Cross—Jesus' death and resurrection
D. The Christ of faith—present with us

Such a christocentric spirituality looks to Jesus as a key to our human search for meaning and happiness. Jesus' identity and importance is implicitly revealed in the "Jesus of history," fully revealed in his death and resurrection, and explicitly articulated in the entire New Testament.

In a sense, the contemporary approach to Christ ends where classical christology began, namely with God.

Both approaches strive to express and preserve the traditional faith of the Church. That faith sees Jesus Christ as "true God" and "true man." For centuries—in creed, catechism, and doctrinal formulations—the Church began with Christ's divinity and moved to Jesus' humanity. Now Christians find it more meaningful to move from appreciation of Jesus as human to an awareness of his divinity. The contemporary approach has also, in fact, been the continual approach of the Church to knowing and loving Jesus Christ through Christian spirituality and art. Ultimately what is at stake is not so much the approach as the attitude motivating the approach. For we are dealing with "faith which seeks understanding." Knowledge of Christ rests finally on love of him. Our study group realized that. We came together to *learn* *about* Jesus, with the best available resources, as a means of getting to *know* him. St. Augustine, one of the greatest of the Church's theologians, expressed well what is most needed in approaching the presences of Jesus: "Give me a lover and he will understand."

PRESENCES OF JESUS

Chapter	Human Experience	Jesus of History	Christ of Faith
1. All-embracing presence	varied experiences many cultures	fascinating, mysterious person	many images many titles
2. Life-enhancing presence	forces of life and death	suffered, died, yet rose to life	Lord, Son of Living God, Life, Word of Life
3. Illuminating presence	search for meaning and purpose	prophet, "the" prophet	Word of God, Light of World
4. Guiding presence	search for happiness, fulfillment	rabbi, teacher	Way, Wisdom
5. Empowering presence	search for security, stability, strength	wonder worker	Savior, Lord
6. Freeing presence	struggle for freedom	messiah, liberator	Messiah (Christ) Savior, Redeemer
7. Mediating presence	desire for reconciliation	man of prayer	Priest, High Priest, Mediator, Son of God
8. Pleading presence	struggle against poverty, injustice	compassionate, caring man	Servant, Suffering Servant, Lamb of God
9. Unifying presence	longing for community, harmony	hospitable to all, bridge-builder	Suffering Servant, Shepherd-King, Son of Man
10. Challenging presence	desire to give and grow	charismatic leader	Law, Model

1

Jesus Christ All-Embracing Presence

I just finished hanging a newly framed "Last Supper" in our dining room. It is not a typical, familiar image like Leonardo da Vinci's famous Last Supper. It is a red, black, green and gold print created by the contemporary Japanese artist, Sadao Watanabe. His depiction of Jesus' final meal with his disciples is highly stylized, authentically Japanese and deeply Christian.

As I look at Watanabe's print, I am drawn to the central figure, Jesus. It is Jesus, but unlike the more familiar pictures of Jesus. He sits on the floor, Japanese style, with his disciples, around a typical, low Japanese table. Watanabe's image of Jesus reflects the traits of Japanese folk art translated into modern print media.

At first glance, Jesus with stylized Japanese features in a Japanese setting, may seem strange. But it is subtly suggestive of who he really is. So, too, is a sensitive painting of Jesus, The Good Shepherd, in which an Indian artist paints Jesus with brown Indian features. I recall a delightful Chinese painting of Jesus blessing the children. Jesus and the children are clearly Chinese. An American Indian Last Supper takes place in a tepee with red-skinned Jesus and disciples. Modern African statues of Jesus reflect the features of black Africans. A charming Indonesian portrayal of Jesus forgiving the adulteress places the scene in a lush tropical forest. Jesus, the adulteress, and the Pharisees have obviously Indonesian features.

These are unfamiliar pictures of Jesus for the average
American Christian but vitally important for our search
into who Jesus Christ really is. These various images of
Christ, all rising out of cultures touched by his presence,
dramatically bring home the all-embracing presences of
Jesus Christ in the world today.

The multiple images of Jesus reveal the profound impact he continues to have on men and women everywhere.
They invite us into the inexhaustible mystery of his identity and importance. It is strikingly suggestive that people so identify with him as part of their lives and culture
that they paint him with their own features. Yet, Christians have done this down through the 20 centuries since
Jesus, a Galilean Jew, lived and died in remote Palestine
and rose to new life for the redemption of all peoples.
Christian art and devotion have created a kaleidoscopic
wealth of images of Jesus, each rooted in authentic experiences of the risen Lord within diverse times and
cultures. Each reveals another facet of who he is.

The earliest Christian art, still preserved in the catacombs, portrays Jesus in the style of Roman art. Early
paintings and statues of Jesus, the Good Shepherd, are
hardly distinguishable from Roman statues of the god,
Hermes, the Roman "good shepherd." The simple art of
the catacombs portrays Gospel scenes of healing and forgiveness. They convey a nobility, a sense of divine
power, mingled with a feeling of human compassion.
Jesus is seen as the Savior, bringing God's healing love
to a broken world. The art echoes the early Christian
creed contained in the still popular symbol of a fish:
"Jesus Christ, Son of God, Savior."

Soon after, as the presence of Jesus became incarnated
in the Greek world centered in Constantinople, the image
of Jesus took on the form of Emperor. Majestic mosaics
reveal a mighty, aloof Jesus inspiring awe before his
power, majesty, and divinity. The godliness of Jesus as
"Pantocrator," almighty ruler of all things, swallows up
the human compassion of the catacomb paintings. Jesus
is worshipped as creator, ruler, and judge, holding the

whole world in his hand. Christians sang in the liturgy of
the time — and millions still sing today in Orthodox
and Catholic churches of the East — "God the holy, God
the strong, God the undying, crucified for us, have mercy
on us."

Just the opposite image grew up centuries later in the
West. Out of a darkened Europe, fragmented and rav-
aged by waves of invaders, Christians gradually created
images of Jesus as helplessly human, sharing the pain
and sorrows of humanity. Francis of Assisi created the
crèche. The crucifix became common, with the wounds
and sorrow of the Crucified evoking compassion and
sympathy. The crown of thorns replaced the crown of
glory. People of the time prayed—as do thousands today
who make the *Spiritual Exercises* of Ignatius Loyola—
feeling "sorrow with Christ in sorrow, anguish with
Christ in anguish, tears and deep grief because of the
great affliction Christ endures for me."

As the Renaissance filled Europe with the rediscov-
ered classical Greek and Roman ideas of beauty, harmony, and balance, Christians created attractive images
of a handsome Jesus, beautiful in body and sensitive in
spirit. Jesus was pictured as the ideal man. He does not
overpower with majesty, nor evoke sympathy for vulner-
ability, but attracts through love and beauty. As Teresa
of Avila wrote, "Although he is my Lord, I can talk to
him as a friend."

In more recent times, after a period of trite, overly sen-
timental portraits of Jesus, modern images of Jesus
reflect the triumphs and tragedies of our times. They
reveal the rich cultural diversity of a pluralistic world
grappling for liberation and for the very meaning of life.
Jesus is seen as deeply identified with human loneliness
and pain, yet overcoming anxiety and anguish through
his inner powers of resurrection. He is a man of sorrows
in a broken world, but triumphing over pain and death,
somehow bridging the apparent gulf between God and
the world. Great religious artists like Georges Rouault
and Marc Chagall show us a suffering but transcenden-

tally peaceful Christ at the very center of the world's prejudices, persecutions and injustice. He, one of us, opens up meaning and hope, freedom and love.

The contemporary artists' image is echoed in the Church's teaching at Vatican Council II: "Through Christ and in Christ, the riddles of sorrow and death grow meaningful" (*The Church in the Modern World,* 22). In him "can be found the key, the focal point, the goal of all human history" (10). In him, life's deepest meaning and potential is revealed.

The all-embracing presence of Jesus Christ as the key to life's mystery is visually evident in the creative works of Christian artists in every age and culture since he promised, "And know that I am with you always, until the end of the world!" (Matthew 28:20). Jesus as a Greek emperor, a Roman shepherd, a Chinese wiseman, a Japanese host, an Italian nobleman, a Flemish merchant, a Spanish gentleman, an African tribal leader, an American Indian chief—all suggest the Christian conviction that Jesus Christ intimately associates himself with the strivings of every human heart in every human situation.

Have you ever seen a Buddha with blond hair and blue eyes? Or a Confucius as a native American? Or Muhammed as an Italian nobleman? While in no way underestimating the validity and authenticity of the other world religions, Christians believe that ultimately the meaning of life is found in the life, death and resurrection of a single man, Jesus of Nazareth, who remains vitally present to men and women of every age and culture.

He identifies with people in all of life's experiences, good and evil, joyful and sad, death-dealing and life-giving. His are the tears of the sorrowing and the smiles of the elated. His are the work of the laborer and the creativity of the artist. His is the love of lovers, friends, and all who open their hearts to those who need them. He it is who is visited in jails, fed at home or in soup kitchens, clothed by parents or social workers, freed in all the world's liberation struggles.

He can be known as a king or servant, teacher or pupil,

healer or sufferer, prophet or clown, criminal or judge, friend or lover, vanquished or victor—for he is so fully identified with all in human experience. "For by his incarnation the Son of God has united himself in some fashion with every person" (*The Church in the Modern World*, 22). In his Spirit he is at work in the hearts and minds and bodies of all men and women everywhere.

It is this all-embracing presence of Jesus Christ that is the unique mystery of Christian faith. Jesus, the Christ, is not just a memory, nor a myth, but a very real individual. We know more about him that is historically certain than we know of the Buddha, Muhammed, Confucius or Zoroaster. We can pinpoint within several years when he was born and when he died. We know he was a Jew who grew up in Nazareth, a village in northern Palestine.

He was for many years a carpenter, and for all too short a time, a wandering storyteller, a challenging prophet and a charismatic healer. We know in bold strokes how he lived and in considerable detail how and why he died in Jerusalem in the prime of his life. We know the core of his remarkable teaching and are reasonably sure of some of his actual words.

Yet who he is, what he is like, continually eludes our grasp. We are continually forced to ask ourselves the very question his first friends asked each other: "What sort of man is this?" (Matthew 8:27). His insistent question to these same friends echoes in our hearts: "And you . . . who do you say I am?" (Matthew 16:15).

Who is this man who lived so long ago in a then remote part of the Roman Empire, whose life spanned such a short time, yet who has been experienced as present by millions of men and women in every part of the globe for over 200 decades? If ever we thought we could adequately sum up an answer in a neat philosophical definition, the Christian art of the centuries makes us pause in wonder. Even the New Testament gives us no single image of Jesus, but rather a rich panoply of names and titles: *Savior, Lord, King, Servant, Messiah* or *Christ,*

Word, Lamb, Priest, Truth, Light, Life, Way, Bread, Son of Man, Son of David, Son of God.

The key to a deeper knowledge of this unique man whose life is mingled with that of every human being is to open oneself to the wonder and mystery of his memory and his presence. We believe he is present with us "always and everywhere" in each moment of our lives. His presence with us is the deepest reality of the most commonplace and most sublime of daily experiences. He invites us to discover his presence in our lives and open ourselves to him. "Here I stand, knocking at the door. If anyone hears me calling and opens the door, I will enter his house and have supper with him, and he with me" (Revelation, 3:20).

Sensitivity and openness to the presence of Christ with us in our daily experience is encouraged by prayerful reflection on his memory. The New Testament, particularly the Four Gospels, is the major source of our memories of him. So it is vital that we open the Scriptures and read about him as we search to discover him in our contemporary world. We need to read the Gospels in the light of our changing experience, and learn to interpret our experience in the light of the Gospels. In this way, day by day, we may come to know him more intimately as present with us, to love him more deeply, and to follow him more closely.

Christian art of the centuries can be an additional help in appreciating his all-embracing presence. For it reveals the profound faith of men and women of many ages and cultures who experienced his presence in their lives. Helpful, too, are the lives of those for whom the presence of Christ was so real as to free them to live as he lived, giving themselves in compassionate service of others. Vitally important are the Church's authentic teachings about Jesus and the liturgical celebration of his memory and presence.

In the following chapters we will explore other dimensions of Christ's presence — life-enhancing, illuminating, guiding, challenging, pleading, freeing, mediating, empowering, and unifying. We will draw upon experience and the rich resources of the Church's living tradition in an effort to discern more deeply who he is and most important, who he is *for us*. We will probe the presences of Jesus.

2

Jesus Christ Life-Enhancing Presence

A woman lay dying on a rough board in a cold barracks at Dachau surrounded by other coughing, crying prisoners. A harried doctor, also an inmate, bent over her. The old Jewish lady looked up.

"How are you today?" he asked. Her eyes lit up. She smiled.

"How can she be smiling," the doctor thought, "in her condition, in this hell-hole?" She glanced up over his shoulder, toward a small window high up in the wall. The doctor followed her glance and, through the window, saw a branch with a green leaf.

"I've been listening to that leaf all morning," she whispered. He bent lower, worried that she was hallucinating. "The leaf was talking to you?" he asked. "Yes." A smile softened her painworn face. "What did the leaf tell you?" Very softly she confided, "Over and over it said: 'Life . . . life . . . new life.'"

Soon after, the old woman died. The doctor, Victor Frankl, survived and became a world famous psychiatrist. He recalls this moving experience in his book, *Man's Search for Meaning.* He was touched by her faith, a faith that could find signs of life even in so deathdrowned a place as Dachau. She could smile in death's face, recognizing the life-giving word of the living God in a green leaf blowing gently in the golden sun.

Her God, the God of Abraham, Isaac, and Jacob, is a God of life. Her scriptures assured her that the living

God breathes life into every living being as he did in the
first moments of creation (Genesis 1: 2). His spirit continues to blow new life into dead, dry bones in Dachau as
he did in Babylon (Ezekiel 37). From his throne flow living waters to bring life to the barren desert (Ezekiel 47).
His word to his people, now as in the past, is: "Live, and
grow like the grass of the fields" (Ezekiel 16:6). Her God,
as the Jewish prophet, Jesus of Nazareth, put it, is the
"God of the living, not of the dead" (Mark 12:27).

Out of this profound Jewish faith in the living God
comes our Christian faith. Jesus grew up in that faith, as
did all his earliest disciples. He and they knew God as
the giver of life. He, more than they, recognized signs of
God's enlivening presence in every living thing: the
birds in the air, the flowers in the field, the people in the
marketplace.

Jesus and his friends wandered from village to village
calling people to open their hearts to the living God,
whose reign was the source of renewed life. Wherever he
went, his words and actions seemed to brim over with
the life-giving power of the living God. Where there was
suffering, he healed. Where people wept, he comforted.

He fed the hungry, gave sight to the blind, cleansed
lepers, calmed the anxious. He reconciled those bur-
dened by sin. He ate and drank with sinners who were
shunned by devout Jews. He spoke words of hope, of ex-
pectancy. Wherever he went, there was an upsurge of
vitality, a deepening and enriching of life. People who
met him with openness experienced through his words
and actions the life-giving force of the God of the living.

It all ended abruptly. Condemned, crowned in
mockery, crucified, he died. His scarred body was lifted
from the cross and laid in a tomb. The tomb was sealed.
It was over. He who brought so much life to others, was
himself dead.

Not surprisingly, those closest to him, those who so
believed him and his message of life, were crushed. Con-
fused, fearful for their own lives, they hid in a locked
room, or slipped out of the city to the safety of more

remote villages. Their lives were drained of meaning, of vitality. Jesus, whom they loved, who had become the center of their lives and hopes, had been executed. He was dead.

But then something else happened, something that reignited a spark of life in this frightened, disoriented group of disciples. That life-spark erupted into a flame that lit up the whole known world. Exactly what happened has been disputed from the moment those disciples pushed open the locked door and boldly preached their "good news."

What did happen to change these frightened fishermen into courageous, charismatic leaders? How could a man who was executed as a political rebel in a remote outpost of the Roman world become the source of renewed life for millions? What difference does what happened then make to us today?

The earliest report we have of what happened after Jesus' death is in Paul's first letter to the Christians at Corinth (I Corinthians 15:1-9). In all probability the words—which are not originally Paul's but are an earlier catechetical or liturgical formula—date back to the early 30s, a few years after the crucifixion.

The tradition Paul hands on is that Jesus rose from death and was seen by many disciples. Paul claims Jesus appeared to him as well. The tradition is as simple as it is startling: Jesus, who was crucified, is alive. This Easter *kerygma* is echoed in other early hymns and acclamations, like "The Lord has been raised! It is true! He has appeared to Simon" (Luke 24:34).

More descriptive is the beautiful hymn to Christ quoted by Paul in Philippians 2:6-11. The sermons of Peter and Paul in the Acts of the Apostles center on the core conviction: "You put to death the Author of life. But God raised him from the dead, and we are his witnesses" (Acts 3:15; see also 2:22-36; 5:30-32; 10:34-43; 13:26-31).

The basic proclamation that Jesus was alive, raised by God to new life, is filled out in the Gospels by the stories of the empty tomb and the stories of Jesus' appearances. Both traditions are independent of each other and are filled with inconsistencies. The tomb-stories apparently arose in Jerusalem, while the appearance-stories seem to have originated in Galilee. The Gospel of Mark was the first to unite these two traditions.

That the tomb was found empty seems historically probable since the fact was easily verifiable and was never denied even by early Jewish adversaries. But the empty tomb remains an ambiguous sign. More important are the appearances of the risen Jesus. That certain disciples of Jesus had real experiences—not just hallucinations, dreams or subjective illusions—also seems historically probable. Something clearly happened to them, something totally unexpected, something outside themselves.

What happened, they insisted, was that they experienced Jesus' presence after his death. He was alive. Their stories dramatically stress that it was really Jesus who appeared to them. It was not a ghost, but the same person they knew and loved before he died. They recognized him. To emphasize the realness and sameness of Jesus, the stories embellish what were visual experiences with reports of touching Jesus, speaking, and eating with him.

Their stories make it equally clear, though, that he was not just the same. He did not just come back to life, like Lazarus, only to die again. He was different now. At first, they did not recognize him. He had entered a whole new kind of life, a new mode of existence which transcended the boundaries and limitations of physical laws.

No one need believe these incredible stories. There is no way to prove that Jesus, in fact, rose from the dead. Yet there is no shred of evidence that his resurrection was a case of psychological delusion, mass hysteria, or a shrewd conspiracy. The witnesses stood by their claim even to the point of dying for it.

What is evident and historically verifiable is the remarkable unleashing of new vitality in their lives. This

small band of fearful, poorly educated, selfishly am-
bitious fishermen was transformed into fearless,
generous, effective leaders, who experienced new life and
attributed it to the presence of the risen Christ.

Others experienced the same life-enhancing presence.
The early communities of believers knew the risen Christ
in "the breaking of bread," the eucharistic meals they
shared in their homes. They experienced forgiveness
through faith in his forgiving presence. Some were
healed in body and spirit through the power of his name.
The growing communities sensed his vital presence in
the fellowship of love they experienced. Despite exclu-
sion from the synagogues and from public office, despite
ridicule and persecution, they exuded a compelling vitality that attracted many.

As the years went on, the Christian communities
reflected on their experience in the light of the Hebrew
Scriptures. They saw signs of new life all around them
whenever people opened their hearts to the risen Christ.
They recalled how everywhere Jesus went before his
death similar signs of life were experienced. They noticed
in his earthly life and in his risen presence the same life-
giving traits their Scriptures attributed to the living God.

Before long they found themselves calling upon Jesus
with the name they had reserved solely for God. "Jesus
Christ is Lord!" they confessed (Philippians 2:11). They
recalled his intimacy with the Father and came to call
him, in a unique sense, the "Son of the living God!"
(Matthew 16:16). They experienced the life-giving presence of God in Jesus' presence with them.

They claimed he was alive with the life of God, that he
had become a "life-giving Spirit" (I Corinthians 15:45).
They called him God's Word (John 1:1-5), the "word of
life" (1 John 1:1). "Whatever came to be, in him, found
life" (John 1:4). From him flowed "rivers of living water"
(John 7:38), life-giving waters, the Spirit. They came to
realize that he came "that they might have life and have
it to the full" (John 10:10). For he was "the resurrection
and the life" (John 11:25).

Men and women today, as in every age since the crucifixion, claim to experience the life-enhancing presence of the risen Lord. They experience the reality of his promise: ". . . know that I am with you always, until the end of the world" (Mathew 28:20). People, open to his presence, continue to find new life even in the many forms of death that envelop them. They affirm that they share the experience of Paul: "Christ is living in me" (Galatians 2:20). His presence with them enables them to live richer, fuller lives.

Vatican Council II confirms the experience of millions of Christians. The bishops state: "Christ has risen, destroying death by his death. He has lavished life upon us . . ." (*The Church in the Modern World,* 22). It is our privilege to "follow Christ who is the principle of life" (52). He is not only the key to penetrating the mystery of life, but the deepest source of life. With him, even death contains the seeds of new life.

As Christians, we share the deep faith of the Jewish woman dying at Dachau, but we perceive the life-giving God through the prism of the risen Christ. Our faith, like hers, opens to God as ever the giver of life. But our faith sees the fullest realization of God's life-giving presence in the presence with us of the risen Lord.

We, too, can look through the windows of death and diminishment and see in a sun-bathed green leaf a sign of new life and of victory over death. But in the leaf's message, we hear echoes of the "word of life," the risen Lord, quietly assuring us: "Life . . . life . . . new life . . . eternal life."

3

Jesus Christ Illuminating Presence

"*W*hat I need is a way of seeing in the dark," says the doctor in the play, *Equus.* He captures the felt need of millions. A recent study of successful business men and women uncovered a paradoxical fact. They had achieved valuable, personal and professional goals, but they confessed that their lives lacked meaning and purpose.

A similar study of successful college students turned up similar results. Asked what they felt was their greatest problem, the majority answered that it was a kind of emptiness or darkness. They longed for light along life's ambiguous paths. They searched painfully for some overriding purpose and meaning to their lives.

"What I need is a way of seeing in the dark" expresses a profound contemporary longing. This longing is rooted in the depths of human experience and spans space and time. It is but the modern echo of the blind man's plea: "I want to see" (Mark 10:51).

The blind man speaks for all of us. He speaks more immediately for the people of his own time, the contemporaries of Jesus of Nazareth. The Jews of Jesus' day were searching anxiously for deeper understanding of life as well as liberation from the oppressive Roman occupation government. They yearned for the light of God's gracious presence.

In centuries past, God sent the great prophets to illuminate the meaning of critical situations. The prophets spoke in God's name. They spoke for him. They uttered his word. They reassured the people of God's presence and care. But for some five centuries, Israel had been without a prophet. In place of the prophets came the law and its interpreters, the Scribes. They did not speak God's living word. They studied and interpreted the words of the law and the prophets. For many, the absence of prophets was a sign of God's absence from his people.

John the Baptizer briefly stirred people's hopes that a new prophet had arisen as a sign that God was indeed still with his people. When Jesus overshadowed John, and began to speak with an authority reminiscent of Moses, Isaiah, and Jeremiah, the people happily concluded: "A great prophet has risen among us . . . God has visited his people" (Luke 7:16).

That the people of his time considered Jesus a prophet in the line of Israel's great prophetic figures seems clear from the Gospels. Jesus' disciples told him that at least some of the people called him "one of the prophets" (Mark 8:28). The same impression of Jesus was relayed to King Herod: "He is a prophet equal to any of the prophets" (Mark 6:15). When Jesus made his triumphant entry into Jerusalem, people asked, "Who is this?" The crowds unhesitatingly answered, "This is the prophet Jesus from Nazareth in Galilee" (Matthew 21:11).

There is evidence, too, that Jesus considered himself a prophet. When people identified him as a prophet, he did not refuse the title. On several occasions, he seems to have at least indirectly identified himself with the great prophetic line of Israel. He reminded his skeptical family and neighbors in Nazareth that "no prophet gains acceptance in his native place" (Luke 4:24). When Jesus was warned that Herod wanted to kill him while he was under his jurisdiction in Galilee, Jesus sent word to Herod reminding him that "no prophet can be allowed to die anywhere except in Jerusalem" (Luke 13:33).

Early on in Jesus' ministry, there are indications that he realized he was the great prophet who was to come, the prophet to whom the earlier prophets looked forward. When John's disciples asked him point blank, "Are you 'He who is to come' or do we look for another?" (Matthew 11:3), Jesus responded by citing signs of the presence of God's reign as described by Isaiah—signs evident wherever Jesus was active—"the blind recover their sight, cripples walk, lepers are cured, the deaf hear, the dead are raised to life, and the poor have the good news preached to them" (Matthew 11:5; Isaiah 29:18-19; 35:5-6).

Even earlier, as he began his preaching in the familiar synagogue at Nazareth, Jesus astounded his family and neighbors by applying to himself the prophetic passage of Isaiah: "The spirit of the Lord is upon me . . . He has sent me to bring glad tidings to the poor" (Luke 4:14-19).

Jesus spoke and acted like the prophets of old, but with even greater urgency and compassion. He probed the heights of human greatness and the depths of human depravity. He explored the ambiguity of human experience and saw God involved in all.

He challenged his listeners with disturbing questions that motivated them to take a deeper look at life and at their hearts: "What are you looking for?" (John 1:38). "Which of you by worrying can add a moment to his lifespan?" (Matthew 6:27). "What profit does he make who gains the whole world and destroys himself in the process?" (Luke 9:25). "Who do you say that I am?" (Matthew 16:15).

He told deceptively simple stories—parables—that unmasked the depths of life's meaning. Few human words cut so deeply into what life is all about as the stories of the Good Samaritan, the Prodigal Son, the Rich Fool, the Great Supper, the Pharisee and Publican, the Laborers in the Vineyard, the Marriage Feast, the Talents, the Last Judgment.

All his questions and stories came to a single point: "This is the time of fulfillment. The reign of God is at hand! Reform your lives and believe in the gospel" (Mark 1:15). Everything he said and did was to help people grasp the implications of that all-embracing message. In it is to be found the ultimate meaning of life.

The message of the kingdom or reign of God sheds clear but warm light on the ambiguities of human experience. Jesus insists that God is alive in the world and in every heart, alive with creative force, with compassionate care, offering freedom and wholeness, with genuine possibilities for brotherhood, justice, and a love that embraces enemies as well as friends. No matter how bad things look at times, evil can be overcome. No matter how puzzling and mysterious life may appear, its deepest mystery is the presence of the all-powerful but equally tender God whose proper name is "Father," or more familiarly, *"Abba,"* ("Daddy") who cares for us passionately. Reality is ultimately gracious. God is with us that we may live, grow and be fully free—of sin, of every evil, of death itself.

To accept God's reign and all the riches it embraces, is to find the key to life's meaning and purpose. But to do so requires a childlike spirit. Jesus claimed that only one with the heart of a child can trust enough, be open enough, be surprised enough to believe what life is really all about. Only one with a child's willingness to fall repeatedly while learning to walk would venture onto a way of living based on Jesus' image of God's reign: "Unless you change and become like little children, you will not enter the kingdom of God" (Matthew 18:3).

Wherever Jesus went, people saw signs of the living God's life-giving presence, if they had the eyes of a child. The hidden world of God's reign could open up before their very eyes. In Jesus' presence, the dark forces of nature and of the human heart were laid bare and overcome. Victims of evil and disease were restored to wholeness. Sinners found acceptance, forgiveness, even table fellowship and friendship with Jesus. People experienced the opportunity for a new start. Their lives were enriched in an unprecedented way.

God's word came to life through Jesus' words and gestures. Where he was present, people sensed God's healing, life-enhancing, compassionate presence. He not only spoke about God's reign, he seemed to embody it. It seemed that to accept God's reign meant, in practice, to accept Jesus; to reject him was to close oneself to the kingdom of God.

That Jesus himself recognized his decisive role in the coming of God's kingdom is sensed from the urgency of his words: "The reign of God is at hand!" His consciousness of his unique intimacy with God is sensed from his familiar conversation with God as his Father.

One dramatic parable poignantly suggests his own awareness of how intimately God's reign is tied to his presence and ministry. All three synoptic Gospels record the parable of the tenants, (Matthew 21:33-46; Mark 12:1-12; Luke 20:9-19). In this parable, the landlord sends a succession of servants to the vineyard tenants. They are all ejected forcefully. Finally, as a last desperate effort, the landlord sends his own son. The son is rejected and killed by the tenants.

The Gospels record that those who listened to Jesus clearly understood its point. The servants were the prophets. God was the landlord and the vineyard was Israel. Jesus was the son. So it happened. The son is put to death. Jesus died without honor, outside the city walls, executed as a lawbreaker. Even in dying, he gave evidence of God's compassionate rule. He forgave the repentant thief and even prayed for those who crucified him. But his death seemed to belie his words even to his friends. It appeared that evil had won out. His death left his disciples disillusioned.

Then, to their surprise, they experienced him alive, risen from death. As more and more of them recognized Jesus alive and with them, they began to witness the very same signs of God's rule as when they travelled with Jesus before his death. The sick were healed, cripples walked, sinners found forgiveness. Most of all, they experienced the peace, joy, and love that Jesus had promised as signs of God's reign.

The experience of the risen Lord led the early Christian communities to discover gradually who Jesus really is.

They remembered what he did and said. They reflected on their own experiences. They slowly realized that Jesus not only spoke God's word as a "prophet powerful in word and deed in the eyes of God and all the people" (Luke 24:19), but is also God's creative Word, present with God from the beginning, intimately at one with God (John 1:1-5). As God's Word, Jesus is the fullest revelation of God and the richest revelation of life's meaning and purpose. His love is God's reign!

The Christian communities recognized Jesus as the long-awaited light that illumines life's every darkness. Early in Matthew's Gospel, we read of Jesus: "A people living in darkness has seen a great light" (4:16). Later reflection led to a profound understanding of Jesus as "the light of the world" (John 9:5). He is that light which "shines in darkness, a darkness that did not overcome it" (John 1:5).

Christians slowly made explicit what was already implicit in Jesus' own words and actions: to accept him was to accept God's word and reign. The ultimate meaning of life is found by coming to personal friendship with Jesus Christ. The profoundest light on life's meaning can be found by opening one's mind and heart to Jesus Christ— God's Word, a word of life, which illumines the whole world. The deepest insight into what life is all about comes not through philosophical speculation or legalistic observance, but through knowledge, love and imitation of Jesus Christ.

In more contemporary language, Vatican Council II echoes the convictions of the early Christian communities. "The Church believes that Christ . . . can through his Spirit offer man the light and the strength to measure up to his supreme destiny . . . She likewise holds that in her most benign Lord and Master can be found the key, the focal point, and the goal of all human history" (*The Church in the Modern World*, 10).

Jesus Christ, with us always and everywhere, is the key to the mystery of life. His presence is an illuminating presence. He hears with compassion the plea of each of us: "What I need is a way of seeing in the dark," just as he was touched by the blind man's cry, "I want to see."

To us, as to the man born blind, Jesus offers new powers to see: "I am the light of the world. No follower of mine shall ever walk in darkness; no, he shall possess the light of life" (John 8:12).

4

Jesus Christ Guiding Presence

*T*he words are haunting and the melody is captivating. The repetition helps you almost taste your yearning for a fuller life. "Lord, teach us to pray ... I've got to find a better way to live ... We lose the way ... Show us the way ... I've got to find a way to really live."

Just after listening for at least the fiftieth time to Joe Wise singing his beautiful song, "Lord, Teach Us To Pray," I happened to pick up the Gospels. Mark tells of a man running up to Jesus and eagerly asking, "Good teacher, what must I do to share in everlasting life?" (Mark 10:17).

The song and the Gospel story touch the same deep chord. They both voice the universal desire to live more fully, more meaningfully, more enduringly. Men and women today respond to Joe Wise's song because deep down it is their song. They can identify with the man in Mark's Gospel, because his poignant question is theirs, too. We all want to find "a way to really live" or "everlasting life."

Joe Wise places this human longing before the Lord, pleading "Show us the way." Mark's questioner turns to Jesus as the "Good Teacher." From Mark's day to our own, millions have come to Jesus in their search for "a better way to live." Then, as now, Jesus was recognized as a "rabbi" or "teacher" who taught the way to life.

The Gospels make it very clear that people saw Jesus as a rabbi or teacher. He is called teacher more than anything else. On several occasions it is recalled that he called himself teacher. He was recognized as a teacher who taught "the way of God in truth" (Luke 20:21).

In many ways he must have seemed like any other young, zealous rabbi. Like them, he gathered around himself a group of dedicated disciples. Like the other rabbis, he taught in the synagogues and, at times, even in the temple in Jerusalem. His teachings, like theirs, found their roots in the Hebrew Scriptures and in the long traditions of his people.

But from the very beginning, he stood out as different. His enemies were quick to point out that he lacked the proper education to be a rabbi (even though they were amazed at his wisdom). He did not himself have a teacher. He had been no rabbi's disciple, nor did he fit any of the various contemporary groups. He was neither a priest nor a theologian. Nor was he a devout Pharisee or an aristocratic Sadducee. He was not a revolutionary Zealot, nor was he a reclusive Essene. He seemed surprisingly unconcerned with the details of legal interpretation, or ritual purity, or the Roman occupation.

Unlike most rabbis, Jesus taught in the fields and hills as well as in the synagogues, in the marketplace and in private homes as well as in the temple. His followers included people with whom the more proper teachers would not even speak: women, children, public sinners.

His words, too, had an originality and freshness that were captivating. He held friend and foe alike "spellbound by his teaching, for his words had authority" (Luke 4:32). Something of the profound simplicity, poetic beauty, and compelling urgency of his teaching can still be experienced in the printed Gospels. He was a master storyteller whose stories still cut to the heart while delighting the mind and imagination. He had the rare ability to help people discover the forest, while others analyzed the trees. Having little time for superficial—even if important—matters, Jesus exposed the inner core of reality. He cut to the fundamental inner attitudes of the heart.

All his teachings were but variations on one profoundly simple theme, a single message that unmasked the hidden depths and riches of life. "This is the time of fulfillment," he proclaimed. "The reign of God is at hand!" That is the "good news" that people flocked to him to hear. To those who listened, he urged, "Reform your lives and believe in the Gospel." Such was his message from the start of his teaching (Mark 1:15).

The freshness and appeal of this "good news" is easily lost on us who have heard it so often and interpreted it so ascetically. For those who first heard Jesus, the message was one of joy, freedom, peace, and fullness of life. His words spoke to people's longing for "a better way to live," for "everlasting life." Those who opened their hearts and minds to his words and God's reign were, as he assured them in the Beatitudes, "happy," "blessed" (Matthew 5:3-12).

In effect, Jesus was saying, "How lucky you are to be alive right now. This is a time of unimaginable opportunity. It is a time full of hope for a better life, a time to get a new start, to really begin to live." It was, he said, "the time of fulfillment." And as he spoke people sensed that somehow the coming of this marvellous time was closely associated with Jesus' words and actions. He seemed deeply conscious of this himself. He was a turning point.

What made this moment so full of potential was the closeness of God's reign or kingdom. "The reign of God is at hand!" God's reign was lifegiving, now, later, always. It was a kingdom of love. In language strange to us, Jesus was saying that God, a God of love, was close by, intimately related to everyone and everything, caring and loyal, that his love was so powerful that no evil power could overcome it. His gracious reign produced peace, justice, truth, respect, love, joy, freedom—everything for which people everywhere longed. Now it was possible.

The reality of God's love was so surprising, so unexpected, so all-embracing, that it was difficult to believe.

Evil seemed so entrenched. The situation appeared so often hopeless. God's reign meant that no matter how much suffering, pain, dying one saw all around, reality ultimately was benign, gracious, loving. It seemed beyond belief. But Jesus said, "Believe it. It's real. Change your way of thinking, reform your lives, take another look."

"Believe the good news," Jesus urged. Accept it like a child. Open yourself to God's love with total trust, like a poor man who can only receive. Trust that you are accepted unconditionally by God, that you are loved no matter who you are. Trust that God's powerful love is the deepest dynamic of all reality. Place yourself in God's hands with total trust. Everything in life is graced by him who is love, whose love can bring life from death. Believe it. Trust him. That is the way to really live.

Then try to live in love. If God so freely loves you, then you are to love others. If he loves with fatherly affection, your love for others must be like that of brothers and sisters. If he forgives you, forgive your neighbor. If he accepts you, accept others. If God responds to your needs, be responsive to other's needs. Treat everyone the way God treats you. That is the better way to live. That is the inner attitude that can transform a world of greed, lust, hatred to one of fellowship, mutual respect and service, justice and peace. This is the way to fullness of life under the reign of a gracious, generous God.

"Reform your lives," said Jesus. In its utmost simplicity, his plea is: Trust God, believing the good news of his ever-present love, and love yourself and everyone as God continuously loves you. This is his "better way to live."

What Jesus taught, he lived. He placed his life totally in the hands of his Father and dedicated all his energies to bringing love to everyone in need.

Jesus went out of his way to find those in need of healing, forgiveness, love. He was often found in the company of people who were known public sinners, such as prostitutes and the despised tax collectors. He sat at table and shared meals with such persons, a sensitively symbolic act that suggested their fellowship with him and with God. This was a scandalous thing for a rabbi to do.

Jesus' actions were as much a part of his teaching as were his words. Even more dramatically his actions expressed the basic message of God's reign of love and forgiveness. Jesus broke the Sabbath proscriptions to bring healing. He proclaimed sins forgiven. He showed considerable freedom regarding legal and ritual purity. He excoriated the more legalistic religious teachers who put law above love, ritual above compassion, and self-righteousness above humble gratitude.

His teachings and lifestyle brought him into sharp conflict with those who claimed to be more orthodox teachers. Opposition to him and his teachings mounted steadily. It became dangerous for him to appear in public, especially in Jerusalem. Jesus knew his life was in danger. Yet he continued to teach God's message of love. He continued to bring healing and forgiveness to those who seemed outside the pale of God's laws. Even when he had been taken by force, falsely accused, condemned unjustly, nailed to a cross of shame, he still loved, and continued to trust. He lived what he taught even to the moment of death. "Father, forgive them," he prayed for those who were killing him; "Father, into your hands I commend my spirit."

Jesus' life and death give tangible shape to his message of God's reign, a reign of unbelievable generosity and love, extending forgiveness and compassion even to one's enemies. Yet, in the end, Jesus died. His way seemed to lead to death rather than to the fullness of life he promised. Evil appeared to win out after all. The power of God's love seemed stifled by the violence of human hatred. It is not surprising that his disciples were disillusioned. We can hardly blame them for sadly looking elsewhere for a way to really live.

But on the third day, Jesus' friends experienced him with them again, fully alive, alive now with a fullness of life that could not be contained. To the two disheartened disciples walking to Emmaus, Jesus pointed out that the only way to life—for the Messiah and for all—was through death. The seed must die to itself if it is to spring forth with new life. All death contains within it the seeds of new life. God's reign does overcome evil, bringing life even from death.

As the years passed, the disciples and the communities that grew up around them reflected Jesus' teachings as they faced new situations, new challenges. They continued to experience the presence of the risen Lord in the power of his Spirit. Gradually, they began to realize that Jesus' "way" to life was found not just in his remembered words, but primarily through union with him. They came to know that he was not just a unique Teacher of God's way, but he was himself "the way" (John 14:6). He not only taught God's reign of love, but that gracious kingdom was realized in his own total trust in his Father and unhesitating love of everyone he met.

The early Christian communities slowly realized that Jesus remained with them in his Spirit as a guiding presence. His way or law was his gracious presence. He was the ultimate criterion of how to live. They felt an urgency not just to learn his teachings but to live like him, to reproduce in their lives the thrust, the quality and direction, of his life, in new historical situations. The way to life was to let his attitude of trust and love become their own attitude. It was not a matter so much of laws and rules as of sensitivity and responsiveness to his guiding presence, to the movements of his Spirit. "The love of Christ impels us" wrote St. Paul (2 Corinthians 5:14).

Today Christians, and the official Church as well, are experiencing anew the guiding presence of the Lord, risen to fullness of life and with us in his Spirit, the Spirit of Love. He is with us to show us the "way to really live," by undertaking to form in us his own attitude of trust and love. The way to life is learned not so much from rule books as through spiritual discernment. Discernment, discovery of the way in concrete circumstances, is the outcome of love and union with the risen Christ, who teaches us through his loving Spirit.

Jesus not only was the "teacher of God's way" in ancient Palestine; he remains the teacher today wherever we may be. His guiding presence, illuminated by his recorded words and example, is the surest way "to really live." He alone can truly fill our yearning for the way to a fuller, richer life. He alone is the Way.

5

Jesus Christ Empowering Presence

"*M*y ship is so small and the sea so large!" I have seen these words so often engraved or painted on polished pieces of marble, on wooden wall plaques, or on prayer cards suitable for mailing or framing.

The words paint a picture of a profound human feeling, an enervating sense of helplessness and fear in the face of threatening powers that seem beyond our control. We are surrounded by destructive forces in nature—hurricane winds, parching sun, flooding, engulfing waters, quaking of the earth. Natural disasters snuff out lives in a few brief moments. Then, too, there are the powers of our own creation that seem to control us. In a world of impersonal computers, deadly nuclear warheads and gigantic multi-national corporations, it is not surprising that people feel helpless.

But the threats are not just from powers outside us. Deadly disease can eat away our very lives from within. An even more frightening sense of helplessness comes from the buffeting force of our innermost impulses. A look into our hearts, or a glance at the morning paper reveals our fragility against the relentless tides of selfishness, greed, lust, anger, hate.

Even with the gigantic strides of the modern physical and social sciences and their related technologies, most of us, at some time or other, experience a profound sense of the world being out of our control. We may even wonder if there is any control, any direction, to this chaotic world. "My ship is so small and the sea so large."

To open the pages of the Gospels is to find them peopled by people like us, sharing a sense of helplessness and hopelessness against seemingly senseless powers of destruction. We read about the sinner caught up in an unbreakable web of temptation, the poor crushed beneath harsh, irreversible economic forces, the sick beset by unknown powers of death, the mentally ill whose emotions seem bent on self-destruction, the possessed in whom the very powers of evil seem to make their home.

It is to these that Jesus raised his voice and reached out his hands. These are the people who turned to Jesus with increased expectation as his reputation spread throughout Galilee and Judea. They brought to him the many tortured shapes and cries of human helplessness and fear. "If you will do so, you can cure me" (Mark 1:40). "My little daughter is critically ill" (Mark 5:23). "My son is possessed by a mute spirit" (Mark 9:17). "Jesus, Son of David, have pity on me!" (Mark 10:47). "Lord, save us! We are lost!" (Matthew 8:25).

Touched by their anguished pleas, Jesus responded with quiet strength and deep compassion. He spoke strong words, words of faith and hope. "This is the time of fulfillment," he said over and over. "The reign of God is at hand!" (Mark 1:15). "Get hold of yourselves! Do not be afraid!" (Mark 6:50).

In language familiar to his listeners, Jesus was saying that God's powerful love was breaking into the world with the force of a new creation, giving life ultimate direction and purpose. The power of evil was being radically broken under the creative power of a caring God. Somehow, he implied, the coming of God's reign of justice, peace, wholeness and love was being initiated through his words and actions. Believe it, he urged. It's good news. Don't be afraid. Everything is not out of control. Love is directing, guiding, controlling all. The Father's care and might extend even to the fragile sparrows. How much more then, to his sons and daughters! (Matthew 6:26–34).

That was the message he never tired of preaching. People found encouragement, hope, strength in Jesus' words. They also noticed remarkable signs that bore out the truth of his words. In Mark's Gospel, Jesus' first words about God's reign are immediately followed by a "miracle story."

At Capernaum, in the synagogue, a man possessed by an evil spirit confronted Jesus. With a single sharp rebuke, Jesus broke the power of the demonic spirit. After a violent convulsion, the man was whole and at peace. Everyone was amazed. "What does this mean? A completely new teaching in a spirit of authority! He gives orders to unclean spirits and they obey!" (Mark 1:23-28).

And so it happened in the scattered towns and villages of Galilee and Judea, even in the bustling city of Jerusalem. Wherever people came to him with trust, the Gospels record a variety of remarkable happenings, always related to Jesus' preaching of God's reign. They are sometimes called "works," or "acts of power"; at other times, they are called "signs." Curiously, these significant actions are never called "miracles" in the Gospels, although that was a common term in the Greek world of the time.

Blind people found their sight restored. Sinners were not only forgiven, but empowered to change their lives. Storm winds and waves were calmed. Demons were driven out. Water became wine. A few loaves and fishes increased to feed a multitude. Jesus walked on the fearsome waves.

People could see and feel the reality Jesus preached. The creative power of God was in their midst in a dramatic way. They were amazed and praised God for giving such power to a man.

After decades of intense research and sharp skepticism, today's Scripture scholars agree that there is a definite historical base for the miracle stories. There is no justification for dismissing them from the Gospel story, for they belong to the earliest strata of the Gospel traditions. Jesus' miraculous deeds actually fill about half of Mark's entire Gospel.

There is little doubt today that Jesus of Nazareth cured people in a manner that caused amazement to those present. He gave evidence of powers over evil forces in people's lives, forces then identified with demons. Only the "nature miracles" seem to lack solid historical basis, as we shall see later. That Jesus did remarkable deeds which caused even his greatest critics to pause in wonder and amazement seems historically certain. Jesus was a "miracle worker" as surely as he was a teacher or preacher.

Unlike other wonder workers of his time—Rabbinic and Hellenistic miracle stories of cures, exorcisms, and other wonders abound—Jesus' signs were motivated by genuine compassion and directed to faith in God. To those who believed, Jesus' miracles were dramatic signs of God's caring power breaking through to overcome the fearful forces of evil: the deadly powers of nature, the diminishing powers of sickness and sin, the awesome powers of the superhuman, the demonic.

Where there was no faith, he could work no signs. In a climate of faith, his amazing deeds turned people's eyes and hearts to God. Powerless persons experienced through Jesus' words and hands a healing, creative, re-newing power. God's loving might was touching and transforming their lives through what Jesus said and did. Through his signs, God's powerful creative love was becoming visible. God's reign—for those who trusted— was the "healing of creation" (Küng).

Not all opened their hearts and minds in trust. Jesus' signs remained ambiguous. Hostile hearts saw in them the power of Beelzebub, the prince of evil. Skeptical minds might cite stories of the many other wonder workers who allegedly healed the blind and lame, raised the dead, changed water into wine. Those with political and religious power might view this wonder worker and his amazing acts as a threat to their own position as well as to God's kingdom.

In fact, not everyone praised God at the sight of Jesus' miracles. What to many were joyful signs of God's creative, caring presence, for others were foreboding signs of opposition to God's rule. In the struggle that ensued, it must have appeared that the hostile skeptics were right. Jesus was successfully silenced. There was an end to his signs. His promise of God's creative presence turning back the forces of evil and death seemed contradicted as he hung dying on the cross, executed out of hatred and fear.

The darkness of Thursday night and Friday afternoon symbolizes the apparent triumph of evil. Even Jesus felt abandoned to the full onslaught of evil forces beyond his control. For him, too, the ship was small and the sea so large as to engulf him. With his body, the hopes and dreams of many were buried in the dank tomb.

But then, on the third day, early Sunday morning, the tomb was found empty. A handful of his closest friends claimed to experience him alive. They believed God had raised him up, overcoming even the power of death. Life had triumphed over death; love had overcome hate. The reign of God was indeed in their midst. The world was not out of control or beyond control. Love and life were the deepest dimensions of existence and commanded persistent direction and purpose.

In the weeks and months that followed, more and more people shared the experience of the risen Jesus. The disciples realized to their surprise that in his name, through his creative power, they performed signs similar to his—healing, exorcising, overcoming the powers of evil. They reflected on their experiences in the light of what they remembered Jesus doing and saying. They prayed and pondered the Hebrew Scriptures, trying to make sense of it all. They celebrated Jesus' creative, healing presence with them as they "broke bread" together in their homes.

By this process of experience and reflection on it in the light of their scriptures and personal memories of Jesus, the small communities of Christians gradually came to believe that Jesus was more than a compassionate, powerful worker of signs of God's mighty care. They found themselves speaking of Jesus in words faithful Jews had used only when speaking of the one God. The remarkable actions of Jesus of Nazareth, which had caused amazement and praise of God, now seemed to draw similar praise to him, risen and alive.

It was not long before the Christians came to call Jesus "Savior," in the sense that they called God their savior. It was no accident that his very name, Jesus, meant "God's salvation." The Christians came to believe that Jesus was more than a prophet or herald of God's healing love.

They remembered his compassion, his concern for those who came to him in pain and fear. They sensed that in Jesus they experienced God's healing, creative presence. They called him, like God himself, their savior, the savior of the world. John writes this post-resurrection faith into the early days of Jesus' ministry as he has the Samaritans say, "We know that this really is the Savior of the world (John 4:42).

They even came to call him "Lord," the name reserved in the Greek translation of the Hebrew Scriptures to the one God. "Jesus Christ is Lord," became one of the earliest Christian creeds (Philippians 2:11). To the believing Jew "Lord" meant—and means— that God is master of the universe, lord of history, holding all reality in existence, giving it direction and purpose with power placed always in the service of love. Fully aware of what they were doing, the young Christian communities called Jesus "Lord," and confessed that "in him everything in heaven and on earth was created. . . . In him everything continues in being" (Colossians 1:15–20). Henceforth nothing could forcibly separate them from God's love in Christ Jesus (Romans 8:35–39).

Out of this post-resurrection faith the Gospels were written. The historical signs worked by Jesus of Nazareth were embellished and multiplied. Cures and exorcisms were "blown up" in detail to bring out what

Christians now believed about Jesus. The "nature miracles"—walking on water, stilling the storm, changing water into wine, multiplying food to feed thousands—were created out of Old Testament themes to identify Jesus with God, the loving Lord of creation and history. Occasioned perhaps by historical events, they became dramatic signs of his creative, healing power over the forces of evil.

In the risen Lord and Savior people found hope and courage, then and over the centuries. Today we continue to experience his healing, creating presence. In him, millions continue to find the power and strength to grapple with the most frightening forces of evil. In him, they find hope and strength when things seem most out of control.

"My ship is so small and the sea so large!" Still true. But the Christian can see Jesus walking on the waters guiding the ship to shore. The Christian may sense Jesus present, seemingly asleep in the boat itself as the crises mount. With such faith, rooted in experience, enriched by remembering the Gospel stories of Jesus' signs, we can say with Paul: "I am content with weakness, with mistreatment, with distress, with persecutions and difficulties for the sake of Christ; for when I am powerless, it is then I am strong" (2 Corinthians 12:10). "In him who is the source of my strength I have strength for everything" (Philippians 4:13).

6

Jesus Christ
Freeing Presence

I once asked a group of sixth graders what slavery was. They told me about slavery in the United States before Lincoln's emancipation proclamation. So I gave them a stack of newspapers and challenged them to see if there were any signs of slavery in the world today. They went to work and to my surprise selected reports of people whose freedom was diminished by poverty, hunger, natural catastrophes, war, political oppression, sickness, drugs, unemployment, ignorance, suspicion, prejudice.

As they talked about what they culled from the newspapers, I asked them what they now thought slavery was and how they felt about it. Their perceptive answer was, "Slavery is selfishness." The conditions the paper reported were symptoms of this inner bondage, a radical slavery that enslaves us all.

Against the reality of this universal bondage and its countless forms of oppression, the reality of Jesus takes on a new meaning. He fully shared the human condition in a time and place that had its own particular kinds of enslavement. Yet to read the Gospels is to discover Jesus as a supremely free person who sets for himself the task of liberating people from all their chains.

Jesus lays out his manifesto of liberation at the very start of his preaching, as described by Luke. In his hometown synagogue at Nazareth, Jesus claims the Spirit of God is upon him, sending him "to bring glad tidings to the poor, to proclaim liberty to captives,

recovery of sight to the blind and release to prisoners"
(Luke 4:18).

This was but another way of stating his *central
message* about the coming of God's reign or kingdom.
God, as the Jewish people learned centuries earlier as
they fled Egyptian slavery, was a God of freedom. Totally free himself, Yahweh set people free. His reign was
liberating.

Jesus was convinced that God's freeing power was
breaking into human experience in a definitive way
through his own words and actions. Wherever Jesus
went, there were signs of God's freeing presence. The
eyes of the blind were opened. The paralyzed and lame
moved freely about. The tongues of the dumb were
loosed, the ears of the deaf unblocked. Those possessed
by evil spirits were freed to lead normal lives. Jesus' miracles were all signs of the liberating reign of God, freeing
people *from* physical, emotional or cosmic-demonic
forces, liberating them *for* wholeness and fellowship.

The bonds that shackle people are not just those of
disease and demons, not just physical and cosmic. There
are enslaving chains forged in the human heart as well.
Jesus knew the slavery arising from oppressive economic forces. As a poor man himself, he experienced
exploitation by the rich and powerful. He felt the burden
of unjust taxation, inflated by the graft and greed of the
tax collectors. So it was natural that Jesus preached
glad tidings of liberation to the poor.

Standing among the poor, as one of them, Jesus spoke
against the corrupting power of money. He courageously
condemned the rich who exploited the poor. Yet he was
no economic reformer in our modern sense. He advocated no plan for more equitable land distribution,
higher wages or lesser taxes. He spoke to the poor about
their dignity and worth as daughters and sons of the
Father. He told them of God's constant care. He assured
them that God's justice was soon coming.

Jesus put his finger on what keeps both rich and poor
in bondage, what creates unjust economic institutions

and exploitative systems. He spoke of the enslavement of the heart to riches, to self-serving security, to selfishness. Such attachment closes one's heart and hands to the needs of brothers and sisters.

Giving, he said, is better than taking, sharing more freeing than hoarding. Jesus' key to economic liberation was not in the realm of economics but of the heart. Effective, imaginative wars on poverty would arise where there was respect for human dignity, sensitivity to other's pain, a sense of compassion and generosity, true poverty of spirit.

In the political realm, too, Jesus fomented no resolution against the Roman occupation government, although he clearly must have shared the deep Jewish longing for political independence. He may have been familiar with the many radical underground movements dedicated to the overthrow of the Romans. He even chose one such radical, Simon the Zealot, as one of his 12 closest disciples. But he resisted every temptation to fight the oppressors with military might.

Jesus' most anguishing personal decisions seem to have centered right on this point. People hailed him as the long-awaited Messiah, meaning by that term, the God-sent revolutionary leader who would liberate the people from Roman domination. Jesus knew he had immense popular support. The Gospels condense into one dramatic struggle what must have been a recurring temptation, namely to accept the role of political-military Messiah or freedom fighter (Matthew 4:1–11).

His choice was to work for a deeper liberation of the heart. Whether in the hands of Romans or Jews, rulers or revolutionaries, he believed power tended to enslave. The oppressed all too readily rise up only to become the oppressors themselves. In the kingdom of his Father, there was only one legitimate power, that of love and service. Any other form of power was more enslaving than liberating (Luke 22:24–30).

Jesus went out of his way to preach liberation from any power not rooted in love and mutual service. If you

are forcibly struck, turn the other cheek. If someone
forces you to walk a mile with him, freely walk a second
mile. If he steals your cloak, freely hand over your coat.
Do not hate your enemies, love them. Control not only
your fists, but the anger in your heart. If you live by the
sword, you will die by the sword.

Jesus' plan for political liberation centered in the
heart. When people's hearts are freed for mutual service,
genuine political reform can be created. Love is the only
truly freeing power.

Jesus lived in a country where cultural and religious
prejudices added to the slavery of economic exploitation
and military occupation. Women were deprived of equal
rights in most areas of social, political and religious life.
Their freedom in public situations was severely
restricted.

Jesus' attitude toward women was so free that it surprised even his disciples. He talked in public with
women, like the woman at Jacob's well, something no
devout rabbi or pious layman would think of doing.
Jesus had close women friends, like Martha and Mary.
He welcomed mothers and their children. He shared with
women the deepest mysteries of God's reign.

Jesus' approach to foreigners showed the same
freedom, the same compassionate respect. The Jews of
his time kept foreigners at a discreet distance lest they
be contaminated by them. The Samaritans in particular
found themselves the objects of intense prejudice and
discrimination. Yet Jesus responded with compassion to
a Roman soldier and an unfortunate Greek woman—in
each case responding to deep faith and profound need.
He makes Samaritans the heroes of his most telling
parables, and does not hesitate to approach them.

But Jesus led no movement for equal opportunity for
women and foreigners in the sense of modern social
reformers. His reform movement cut to the heart of the
matter, respect for each person as a daughter or son of
the same Father. All artificial social restraints and prejudices would be overthrown as people freed their hearts

to love and respect others as they loved and respected
themselves.

Jesus was most strikingly free in his attitude to those
considered as public sinners and outcasts from God's
people—tax-collectors, prostitutes, and the like. Jesus
freely associated with them, to the scandal of the priests,
the theologians, and the pious laity. Most shocking of all
was the fact that Jesus ate and drank with them and proclaimed God's forgiveness even to them.

For the Jews of Jesus' time, a meal was more than a
matter of physical nourishment. To eat at the same table
implied fellowship. When Jesus ate and drank with
public sinners, he was expressing his fellowship and solidarity with them. As a rabbi, one sent by God to speak
for God, his meals with sinners affirmed their fellowship
with God. The loving, healing, forgiving reign of God
was indeed within their midst, a rule not restricted by
the religious rules of his people. God was a God of mercy
and forgiveness, demanding mercy more than legal
observance or cultic sacrifice.

Jesus went out of his way to make this point. He freely
violated the many legal and ritual prescriptions that
would have prevented his association with acknowledged sinners. He deliberately violated even the sacred
Sabbath laws to bring healing and forgiveness to those
who were in need. He allowed his disciples to break the
Sabbath to satisfy their hunger. The Sabbath, he told his
critics, was for people. God's reign was for people, for
their wholeness and happiness. Even so sacred a law as
that of Sabbath must bend to respond with compassion
to human need.

Jesus violated religious laws to bring forgiveness to sinners and to dramatize the proper priorities in the Father's
kingdom. Such freedom was seen as a threat to true religion. What was even more unheard of was Jesus' personal
attitude toward the Mosaic law itself. The Law of Moses,
the Torah, was—and still is—respected as God's own law.
Theologians then might vary in their interpretations of
the Torah, but none would dare change a word of it.

Jesus scandalized many by doing just that. He freely
contradicted the Torah on a number of important points:
divorce, oaths, retaliation, the attitude toward enemies
(Matthew 5:21-48). He further interpreted it in a radically internalized form—where the law forbade murder,
Jesus saw God forbidding anger; where the law forbade
adultery, Jesus said God forbade lust. And Jesus made
his corrections to the Torah on his own authority. Not
"thus says the Lord," (as the prophets and theologians
spoke) but "this *I* say to you."

In effect, Jesus was preaching a radical freedom from
every law but the will of God, the law of love. It is not
surprising that Jesus was seen as subversive to the religious establishment. His attitude toward the law, his fellowship with and forgiveness of public sinners were at
the heart of people's growing opposition to him. His
open confrontation with the religious teachers and
authorities intensified their antagonism. Jesus went out
of his way to challenge, criticize, and condemn any approach to religion that placed legal observance or cultic
worship above mutual love, compassion, and forgiveness.

Eventually, the inevitable happened. His opponents
moved to silence him. Captured and condemned as subversive to true religion—a blasphemer who claimed to
forgive sins, a flagrant violator of the law—he was
handed over to the Romans who executed him as a political revolutionary.

His death seemed the end of this attractive, threatening man of freedom. But his disciples experienced the
ultimate power of Jesus' freedom as he broke even the
bonds of death, that last enslavement of sin.

During those early days, they themselves experienced
in his risen presence a remarkable freedom—from fear,
disillusionment, and despair. Gradually, they and their
growing bands of converts found themselves more and
more free of prejudices, from bondage to money and
power. His freeing presence led them to a new freedom
regarding the material world and its riches. Their communities, despite tensions, reflected the mutual respect,

sharing and forgiveness that Jesus said exemplified God's reign of love.

Among them there was no longer Jew or Greek, male or female, master or slave—all these artificial barriers were leveled (Galatians 3:28). They found in mutual love a power that eventually overcame Rome itself, a more liberating power than the sword. They found themselves freed from the Mosaic law and all law except the law of the Spirit of Christ, the law of love, which spontaneously fulfills all other laws that do not stifle the Spirit. They were freed from sin's power.

In every age, Christians have experienced the same freeing presence of the risen Lord and his Spirit. As Paul wrote, "where the Spirit is, there is freedom" (2 Corinthians 3:17). Ultimately, that freedom is a freedom from selfishness which, as my sixth graders perceived, is the most basic form of slavery. "Remember that you have been called to live in freedom . . . Out of love, place yourselves at one another's service" (Galatians 5:13).

7

Jesus Christ Mediating Presence

*T*he two young men knelt on the grass near the Washington Monument. They seemed oblivious of the tourists milling about. One had a crucifix around his neck. He set his worn Bible on the grass by his knees. He placed his arm around his companion's shoulder. They both bowed their heads and prayed in silence.

It was a moving sight, touching in its simplicity. The two seemed to be trying to bridge whatever separated them from each other and from Someone greater. Bent knees, bowed heads, and an arm around a shoulder spoke without words of their inner yearning for communion with the Transcendent and community with each other.

These two men praying so openly in a public place are living icons of the heart's hunger for union and harmony. They are but two of millions, young and old, who turn to prayer in search of a sense of belonging that they cannot find in human effort alone. People today seem profoundly aware of their distance, their alienation from one another and from some deeper source of wholeness. And so they pray.

In their prayerful search for communion and community, people have much in common with Jesus. Gospel evidence clearly shows that he prayed and prayed often. In fact, the Gospels, particularly that according to Luke, portray Jesus as praying habitually. His life was lived in an atmosphere of prayer.

Luke points out that Jesus was in the habit of participating in the synagogue services on the Sabbath

(Luke 4:16). Jesus seems to have prayed regularly at meals according to the traditional Jewish practice (Matthew 14:19). Although the Gospels do not mention it, we may assume that Jesus also prayed the most fundamental daily prayers customary among all devout Jews.

Morning and evening he undoubtedly prayed the *Schema Israel* (Deuteronomy 6:4-5), professing his unreserved love for God with all his heart, and soul and strength. Along with the *Schema,* Jesus would have prayed the traditional prayers of praise and benediction, the *Tephilla.* No doubt he learned these common Jewish prayers at home from Mary and Joseph.

In addition to the traditional prayer practices of his people, the Gospels record some of Jesus' more personal habits of prayer. He prayed for concrete persons, like Peter (Luke 22:32), and his executioners (Luke 23:34). His busy days were interspersed with moments, even whole days or nights, of intimate union with God in prayer. Jesus often slipped off to the mountains or desert for uninterrupted solitary prayer (Luke 5:16). Luke hints that the Garden of Gethsemane was one of the quiet spots Jesus frequently came to for prayer (Luke 22:39).

Particularly at critical moments in his life, Jesus turned to prayer. His public ministry began with a profound religious experience at the Jordan as John baptizes him (Mark 1:9-11). This was followed by an extended period of prayer in the desert, during which he struggles with the meaning of God's call and his own mission (Mark 1:12-13). Before the critically important choice of the Twelve, Jesus "went out to the mountain to pray, spending the night in communion with God" (Luke 6:12). It was after a period of extended prayer that Jesus taught his disciples to pray the "Our Father" (Luke 11:1-4).

As opposition to him mounted and his life was increasingly in danger, Jesus turned still more to prayer. Luke recalls that just prior to Jesus' decision to go up to Jerusalem despite the danger to his life, he went up a mountain to pray. It was there "while he was praying" that he was transfigured before his three closest friends (Luke 9:29). His last days were filled with personal and ritual prayer. And his life ended in prayer on the cross, where his last words may have been the Psalms (Psalm 22 in Mark and Matthew; Psalm 31 in Luke).

Jesus' life was a fabric of prayer. But the Gospels provide only rare glimpses of the content of his prayer. For the most part, the descriptions of Jesus' profound prayer experiences are highly elaborated theological constructions of the evangelists—for example the accounts of the baptism, temptation, transfiguration, and cross. But even these passages which show obvious signs of editorial rewriting no doubt preserve echoes of Jesus' actual prayers.

The Gospels do preserve two examples of Jesus' prayer that seem to be still closer to his actual words. Scholars hear in these two accounts, also retouched by the evangelists, a more authentic, original ring. Both are found at critical turning points in Jesus' life and ministry. Because at these moments he is grappling with the very meaning of his life and mission, these two prayers provide rare glimpses not only into how Jesus prayed, but who he knew himself to be and what he saw as his mission in life.

The first prayer is found as Jesus begins to realize that his popular support has begun to wane. Official opposition to him had been growing. Scribes, Pharisees, Sadducees—the religious leaders of his people—openly challenged his message and mission. But now even the crowds seem to be leaving him. Even in towns "where most of his miracles had been worked" (Matthew 11:20), people were turning away.

At this moment of intense frustration and disappointment, Jesus prays. "Father, Lord of heaven and earth, to you I offer praise; for what you have hidden from the learned and the clever you have revealed to the merest children. Father, it is true. You have graciously willed it so" (Matthew 11:26).

In prayer, Jesus finds reason to praise and thank God
at the very moment when his mission seems to be failing.
If the learned leaders turn against him, at least some of
the simple and childlike respond to his words and works.
Jesus could see something marvellous and gracious happening in what is more and more obviously a doomed
ministry. Jesus sees this as God's doing, as God's will.
God is powerfully active in these events, and his
greatest power is his love. That mighty love can achieve
wonders, bringing success out of failure, good out of evil.
Jesus' prayer of thanks and praise reveals the profound
meaning he sees in his life, a life wholly permeated by
God's loving activity.

Just how intimately Jesus sees himself united with
God is revealed in how he speaks to God. He calls upon
God directly and simply as "Father." It is hard for us
today—so accustomed to praying the Our Father—to
realize how surprisingly original and unique Jesus' use
of the term really was. No text in the Hebrew Scriptures
or in rabbinic writings dared speak to God in such
familiar terms. In fact, reverence for God forbade even
the use of his proper name in Jewish prayer.

Yet Jesus here prays to God as "Father." In his native
language, Aramaic, he goes so far as to address God as
Abba, a term of familiarity, intimacy, affection. It was
used by children talking to their fathers, much like we
use "Dad," or "Daddy."

Praying with such unheard of familiarity, Jesus seems
conscious of a profoundly intimate bond, a warm, loving
relationship or union such as no one else shared. In a
special way he alone can call God *"my* Father" (Matthew
10:32). He seems to experience a communion with God
that is altogether unique, an intimacy that allows him to
praise and thank God not just as "Father" but as "Daddy." *Abba* reveals not only the content of Jesus' prayer
but suggests the mystery of who he is.

A second remarkable account of Jesus' own prayer
takes us deeper into how Jesus prayed and how he saw
his life. On the night before he died, Jesus went off to the

Garden of Gethsemane to pray. He is facing his most severe crisis. He must come to a most difficult decision. He knows that his life is in danger, but that there is still time to escape. Should he continue his ministry of preaching the reign of God and thereby continue unmasking the hypocrisy of the already hostile religious leaders? Or should he retreat back to Galilee and relative safety?

Jesus seems gripped with terror. He fears the torture and possible death that he realizes may be his fate. To his three closest friends he admits, "My heart is filled with sorrow to the point of death" (Mark 14:34). Then totally alone in the darkness he prays over and over, "*Abba* (Oh Father), you have the power to do all things. Take this cup away from me. But let it be as you would have it, not as I" (Mark 14:36).

Still conscious of the intimate bond between himself and God, *his* Father, Jesus experiences human alienation and anxiety to the extreme. His whole being struggles to respond to the Father's will. He experiences the pain, the distance, the unknowing that is so much a part of the human condition. He is so fearful and distraught that he pleads like a child with his Father to find another way.

Yet even in this extreme moment of human distress and decision making, Jesus surrenders himself into the Father's hands. He abandons himself with trust into the hands of God, whom he believes to be totally good and loving. "Amen," he says. "So be it. Your will be done." Jesus responds in obedient love and trust. Having preached the reign of God to others, he now submits to that reign himself in total self-surrender. "Amen, Father. Your will be done."

God, Jesus realizes, does not seek his death. The Father is not angry, but seeks life and love for human beings. He asks his son to continue to show forth in his words and works the Father's compassionate love so that others might find life and healing. Jesus' anguish arises from his realistic assessment of the consequences to him of such a course of action. Trusting in God's powerful love as ultimately life-giving, Jesus chooses to continue the Father's work no matter what the danger or personal cost.

That night, his decision leads to his capture, and to his death the next day. Dying in excruciating pain on the cross, Jesus surrenders himself anew to the Father who now seems to have abandoned him. "Father, into your hands I commend my spirit" (Luke 23:46). Loving to the very end, he prays for those who executed him, "Father, forgive them" (Luke 23:34).

Jesus died as he had lived, a "pray-er." His disciples, and the communities that soon gathered around them, long pondered the constancy and content of Jesus' prayer. Their own lives, like his, centered on prayer (Acts 2:42–46). As they prayed and lived together, they came to experience a remarkable sense of oneness with God and one another. They sensed the presence of the risen Lord with them in his Spirit. The Spirit of Jesus enabled them, like Jesus himself, to pray intimately to God "*Abba,* Father" (Romans 8:15; Galatians 4:6). They sensed that they were, because of Jesus and his Spirit, truly God's sons and daughters, brothers and sisters of the same Father. They felt at one with God and with one another. Distance, alienation, separation had been bridged.

The evident source of their new awareness of communion and community was Jesus and his Spirit. Remembering Jesus' habitual prayer and pondering on its content helped them better understand his role in making possible their experience of "at-one-ment."

The original and unique "*Abba*" of Jesus' prayer shed light on just how intimately united he was with God. He was "Son" as no one else was. In him, the fullness of the Father's grace and glory was visible, tangible, and attractively human. Whoever saw him, actually saw the Father, for the Father was in him and he was in the Father (John 14:9-10). It was the Father's words he spoke, the Father's works he did. The fullness of God's healing, renewing love came to humankind in and through him. He was God's bridge, God's gift, to an alienated humanity.

Yet his unconditional "Amen" to God's will, a "Yes" wrenched out of intense inner struggle, evidenced just how identified with humanity's plight he had become. As no one else was able to do, he gave the fullest possible response of obedient trust to God's offer of love. He surrendered himself totally to the will and grace of the Father. Sharing our pain and unknowing, Jesus spoke as one of us, accepting God's gift of wholeness. He was our bridge to God. In him we had confident, free access to the Father.

Slowly the Christian communities came to the profound awareness that Jesus was the unique mediator between God and people. God's very Son, yet born of a woman, born under the law, he freed people from slavery so that they might share his sonship. The Christians experienced this as they received his Spirit, the "spirit of adoption" (Romans 8:15). In him, the distance between God and people and between people themselves might be bridged.

Late in New Testament times, Jesus, the unique mediator, was given the title "Priest" or "High Priest" (Hebrews 5:7-10). It was a fitting title for one—himself not a Jewish priest—who lived out his mission of mediation in an atmosphere of prayer. Through his prayerful sacrifice, God's grace became freely available. In him, men and women might now approach the God of grace as God's children.

In Jesus, we can fall on our knees, embrace our brothers and sisters, bow our heads and pray, "Abba, Father, your will be done. Amen." Our prayer is taken up in the prayer of Jesus, our Priest. His mediating presence brings the Father to us and opens up our way to the Father.

The two men praying near the Washington Monument evidently believed that.

8

Jesus Christ Pleading Presence

O ne chilly fall afternoon in New York City, I noticed a blind beggar sitting in the sun outside a restaurant. As persons approached him, he raised his voice in a monotonous plea for help. He held out a tin cup. He did not ask for much, just a dime or a quarter.

Fortunately he could not see those who passed. Most hurried by with little more than a passing glance. Some seemed to look the other way. One or two looked back a bit guiltily, but went on anyway. One young tough made an obscene gesture and cursed the beggar. A few stopped, usually without a word, reached into their pockets or purses, and let a couple coins clink into the cup.

It was a sad sight. The blind beggar's pleading voice and outstretched arm haunted me long afterwards. Blind and poor, he was a fellow human being in need. The dull clink of the few coins captured the hollowness of people's response to him.

That pleading man was probably not much different from Bartimaeus of Jericho. Sitting by the roadside one day, begging from the passersby, Bartimaeus learned Jesus was coming down the road. The blind man began to shout, "Jesus, Son of David, have pity on me!" People nearby angrily told him to be quiet. But he shouted still louder, "Jesus, have pity on me!"

Jesus stopped. He looked for the man who was calling out to him. Spotting the blind beggar, Jesus was moved with compassion. He went over to Bartimaeus and asked him what he wanted. The blind man pleaded for sight. Jesus responded warmly to Bartimaeus' faith-filled plea. At Jesus' word, the blind man's eyes were cleared. He was able to see (Mark 10:46-52).

This touching story is a kind of dramatic parable of Jesus' entire life. In Mark's Gospel, the cure of Bartimaeus is the final incident in Jesus' public ministry prior to his entry into Jerusalem one week before his death. This story reveals the deepest motivation of Jesus' life and ministry. It suggests, too, why Jesus, so obviously a good man, was condemned by the religious leaders of Israel. Jesus' compassion led to the cross.

Jesus' sensitive response to Bartimaeus is typical of his entire public life. He was deeply responsive to people in need, the poor and oppressed, the sick and suffering, the anxious and tormented, the hungry, the sinner. He went out to those in need and they searched him out knowing his kindness. There was an evident bond between himself and suffering human beings.

Although he was a devout Rabbi, Jesus was frequently seen in the company of those considered sinful or religiously unworthy. He entered the homes of public sinners, ate and drank with despised tax-collectors and prostitutes. He associated freely with society's rejects and religion's outcasts—the poor, lepers, aliens, cripples, diseased. His sensitive compassion for hurting human beings led him to a kind of solidarity with the needy.

Jesus' identification with the poor was motivated, too, by something more than his sense of human compassion. Jesus responded to the needy not only because he was touched by their suffering, but also out of religious conviction. Jesus believed the mystery of God was accessible only to those who draw near to the poor. In his profound search for ever closer union with God, Jesus searched for him where he believed God was most likely to be found — among the suffering and needy.

He believed God's voice could most surely be recognized in the pleas of the poor. His conviction was rooted in the most traditional teaching of the great Hebrew prophets before him—Amos, Hosea, Isaiah, Jeremiah. The God of the prophets was a God of compassion. He was on the side of the "orphans and widows," and all the helpless, hopeless, pleading people of the world.

Curiously, in the religious orthodoxy of Jesus' time, it was precisely these people who were believed estranged from God and a source of uncleanness to devout Jews. Aliens like Samaritans or Gentiles, lepers and cripples, prostitutes and tax-gatherers, law-breakers and sinners were to be avoided by anyone seriously seeking God's presence. For the religious establishment of the time, God was to be found rather in the temple and synagogue, in observance of the law, in the careful performance of prescribed ritual and sacrifice.

Jesus' compassionate solidarity with the "unclean" was therefore a scandal in the eyes of the religious hierarchy. Jesus' words and deeds challenged the basic teachings of Scribes, Pharisees, Sadducees, and Priests. Contrary to their theology, Jesus taught that the privileged place to find God was precisely among those who were thought estranged from God. Without deprecating the holiness of temple and Torah (Jesus remained to the end a devout, orthodox Jew), he insisted that the all-holy God was to be found first and foremost among people, particularly among those in genuine need.

Out of the deepest religious conviction, as well as from human compassion, Jesus freely identified himself with those considered outside the realm of God's grace. His compassionate lifestyle became a conscious challenge to the most fundamental religious assumptions of the then contemporary theology and orthodoxy.

Jesus' association with the sick and sinful forced people to question and rethink their assumptions about God, about religion, about sin, about holiness. He was saying, in effect, that God was with the poor and the outcast. They were even more his temple than the great temple in Jerusalem. Compassion was the core of the law.

The parable of the Good Samaritan boldly expressed where Jesus stood. A traveller is robbed, beaten, and left half dead along the Jericho road. A priest sees the bleeding body, but passes quickly by. Then comes a levite, an assistant in the temple. He, too, glances at the beaten man, and then goes about his business. There follows a Samaritan—an alien, a hated heretic. He sees the poor victim, is moved with compassion, and responds generously to his desperate need. Jesus' point is clear. Response to someone in need, the definition of "neighbor," is the very heart of the law. Who is observing the law? Not the priest and levite, scrupulous devotees of legal and ritual purity, but an unclean, despised Samaritan (Luke 10:25-37).

It is no wonder that Jesus' teachings and lifestyle led to steadily increasing conflict with the religious authorities. He publicly challenged the prevailing orthodoxy. He angrily unmasked the hypocrisy of those who were using religion, with its legalistic casuistry, to cover up their lack of compassion for people in need. Those with vested interests, as well as sincere convictions, who felt compelled to defend their religious orthodoxy and authority, sought to silence Jesus. His compassion, grounded in human sensitivity and religious conviction, led directly to the cross.

The case against Jesus was essentially religious. Before the High Priest and the Sanhedrin, he is accused of undermining temple worship and observance of the law. He is seen as a false prophet, a fake messiah. The verdict is guilty; the crime is blasphemy; the penalty is death. Jesus is condemned for being against the God of his fathers. Only before the Roman Governor is the charge changed to a political one—insurrection against the emperor.

Now Jesus finds himself in the very situation as the people he had gone out of his way to help. Like them, he is now considered a sinner, outside the realm of God's gracious presence. Devout followers of the law would now have nothing to do with him. He is an outcast like the lepers, the blind, the demented, the aliens with whom he so freely associated. Jesus now experiences a new solidarity with the poor and the suffering. He knows firsthand their helplessness, their need, their pain. He is one of them.

Jesus' painful identification with suffering humanity deepens as Thursday melts into Friday. He is imprisoned, stripped, beaten. Weak with pain, he becomes the object of cheap jokes and mocking laughter. He is led through the streets like a common criminal as people look on with curiosity and horror.

Considered unclean, Jesus cannot even die within the Holy City. Nailed to a cross, he hangs for three hours in excruciating pain. Helpless. Alone. Naked. Thirsting. Utterly poor. One with the needy in his lifetime, he is still more intimately identified with them in death.

Most agonizing of all, Jesus feels abandoned even by his Father. He pleads, "My God, my God, why have you forsaken me?" (Mark 15:34). He who preached God's nearness in grace and love, now begs for some sign of his presence. Jesus experiences God's absence in his extreme suffering, poverty and need. Seemingly abandoned even by God, he shares to the full the feelings of millions who live and die in misery, alienated from more fortunate human beings.

Jesus, who was so compassionate all his life, now stirs compassion himself. A Roman soldier offers him a drugged drink to ease his pain. Mary his mother, John, and a few women stand beside him, suffering with him. When he dies, his weeping friends bury him, and go off to mourn him. His enemies set a guard at his tomb.

Before the weekend is over, the sorrowing disciples are surprised out of their sadness by his presence, alive with new life, victorious over suffering and death. He comforts Mary in her sorrow at the tomb (John 20:11–18). He walks with the distressed, disillusioned disciples on the Emmaus road (Luke 24:13–35). He strengthens the frightened group locked inside the Upper Room (Luke 24:36–49). The descriptions of the appearances of the risen Lord convey the same kind of sensitivity and compassion Jesus showed in his life and ministry.

As the days went by, the disciples and the communities that formed around them experienced in new circumstances the presence of the risen Christ and his Spirit. They rejoiced in his victory over suffering and death, but they never forgot the sufferings of the Crucified. The Spirit of Jesus, whom they recognized as coming to them from the cross of Jesus (John 19:30), led them back to the cross. While they celebrated the victory of the Lamb, they remembered that the victorious Lamb remained always "a Lamb that had been slain" (Revelation 5:6).

They came to realize that the marks of his sufferings were visible all around them. The cross of Jesus was seen in the pain of others. In a mysterious sense Jesus, who had identified himself with the needy in his compassionate life and even more so in his agonizing death, was still to be found in solidarity with people in need. They remembered Jesus' words: "Be compassionate as your Father is compassionate!" (Luke 6:36). The risen Lord was to be met not just in their eucharistic celebrations but in the anguished faces of hurting human beings.

Matthew's account of the final judgment provides a profound insight into the pleading presence of Christ in the monotonous, insistent pleas of suffering men and women. No doubt the account has roots in the words of Jesus himself, but has unquestionably been edited in the light of post-resurrection experience. It provides the surest measure of whether a Christian truly knows Jesus Christ and is following his way. It points to the Lord's hidden, frequently overlooked presence in anyone who suffers, a presence that continually comes as a shock and surprise.

"I was hungry . . . thirsty . . . a stranger . . . naked . . . ill . . . in prison," says the Lord to those on both right and left. Each group asks in amazement when they responded to, or failed to respond to, him in his need. "Lord, when did we see you hungry or thirsty or away from home or naked or ill and in prison . . . ?" The answer is straightforward and definite: "As often as you did it for one of my least brothers, you did it for me ... As often as you neglected to do it to one of these least ones, you neglected to do it to me" (Matthew 25:31–46).

Identified with the needy in life, still more in death, Christ Jesus remains identified with them in his risen life. Access to the compassionate Father and equally compassionate Son is through compassion to people in need, as well as through prayer and virtue.

The voice of a blind beggar pleading for dimes and quarters on a busy city street may well be the pleading voice of Christ Jesus, our Lord and King, who was always found among the blind and poor and alienated.

"Men go to God when they are sore bestead,
Pray to him for succour, for his peace, for bread,
For mercy for them sick, sinning or dead:
All men do so, Christian and believing.
Men go to God when he is sore bestead,
Find him poor and scorned, without shelter or bread,
Whelmed under weight of the wicked, the weak, the
    dead:
Christians stand by God in his hour of grieving."

—Dietrich Bonhoeffer, *Letters and Papers from Prison*

9

Jesus Christ Unifying Presence

*O*ne of my favorite children's books is *Swimmy* by Leo Lionni. Swimmy is a small black fish. He lived in a school of fish like himself, except that they were all red. One day a huge, hungry tuna fish ate the whole school in one big gulp. Only Swimmy escaped.

Sad and afraid, Swimmy swam alone among the dark ocean shadows. Gradually his fright subsided. He ventured out into the sunrays and discovered a fascinating world of living shapes and colors.

Then one day Swimmy came upon a school of little red fish. They were just like him, except that he was black. They were hiding in the deep darkness under plants and behind rocks. They were terribly afraid of the big fish. And with good reason.

Swimmy felt sorry for them, always hiding, fearful of hostile fish. They were missing so much. So Swimmy called them all together. He taught them to swim close together in formation. Swimmy placed himself as their eye. Together they looked like one giant fish moving serenely through the waters. Now they swam freely and happily wherever they wished — without fear of unfriendly fish.

Leo Lionni's charming, beautifully illustrated story provides a penetrating glimpse into the human situation. We are not unlike the frightened little fish, each seeking its own security against massive enemy forces. We know the fear that leads us to hide alone in seemingly safe shadows. We are all familiar with the many divisions that separate us from other human beings. Caught up with suspicion, distrust and fear, we pull back from others, and we build walls of separation between us.

The world Jesus knew firsthand was very much the same as ours, not in its external shape but in its inner experiences. Jesus was constantly meeting individuals who were crippled by anxiety, by alienation. He encountered individuals and groups filled with hostility toward others.

The Jews of Palestine were fragmented by factions of all kinds. One of the few things they all seemed to share was a hostile distance from the Romans who occupied their land. They kept themselves carefully separated from the Romans and from all other non-Jews. Their world was neatly divided among themselves, God's people, and the rest of the world, "the nations." Samaritans were avoided even more than pagans, although the Samaritans claimed to worship the God of Israel.

Among the Jewish people themselves there existed many barriers of separation. Pharisees, devout laypersons, were often at odds with the priestly Sadducees. Hot-blooded Zealots had no time for those who took a more compromising stand toward the Romans than they did. Women lived publicly in a world of their own, unable to sit with men even in the synagogue. Devout Jews carefully avoided "sinners." Slaves moved in different circles than did their masters. Lepers were forced to live in isolation outside the villages. Rich looked down on poor. The powerful oppressed the helpless.

Onto this scene of scattered factions Jesus walked, apparently very much at home with all parties. Looking at the disparate crowds, he saw them "like sheep without a shepherd" (Mark 6:34). He responded to their repressed yearning for unity by overlooking the barriers between them. From his first appearance as a wandering rabbi in his native Galilee, we find Jesus bridging the many existing divisions. He drew people of all kinds to himself, and in the process drew them closer to one another.

This is immediately the case with his closest, carefully

chosen, disciples. In selecting twelve special followers, Jesus was dramatically recalling the twelve tribes of Israel—disparate bands of nomads called to unity by God at Mount Sinai and forged into a "people" under Moses' leadership during the forty years of desert wandering (Exodus 24:3–8). The Twelve Jesus called to share his ministry were themselves a mixed group. Among them were simple fishermen, a learned but despised taxcollector, several ascetic followers of John the Baptizer, at least one revolutionary Zealot, perhaps some workmen or peasants. From these people with diverse backgrounds and points of view Jesus formed a close community of friends, a kind of traveling commune. His presence was the attractive focal point of the community of disciples.

Moving from village to village with these followers, Jesus reached across the multiple walls of prejudice and ill will. He made a special effort to draw to himself in a compassionate fellowship those whom official Judaism at the time considered outside the pale of God's care—tax collectors, prostitutes, lepers, the emotionally and physically handicapped. His stepping over the customary dividing lines between men and women raised surprised eyes even among his friends. He did not hesitate to reach out to Samaritans, or to make them heroes in his parables. A Roman army officer, and a brave Phoenician woman experienced the same gracious power as did devout Jews. Everywhere, to everyone who was open to him, Jesus offered reconciliation and fellowship. The crowds who gathered around him comprised members of the many divisive factions existing in Palestine. His presence was like a catalyst facilitating solidarity.

To the spiritually sensitive, the unifying effect of Jesus' presence must have seemed the first signs of a dream coming true. Jesus' insistent announcement that God's reign was now at hand recalled a dream of unity that recurred in the Hebrew Scriptures. For all Judaism's concern about racial and religious purity, involving separation from all who were unclean, it never lost its primitive vision of a world in which all nations were united in the service and praise of the one God. God was continually at work to gather together, not only the dispersed tribes of Israel, but all the nations of the world as well. The dream was one in which God's house would be "a house of prayer for all peoples" (Isaiah 56:7).

The dream began with God's promise to Abraham to make him "the father of a host of nations" (Genesis 17:1-8). That covenant had a universalist perspective. Called to a special closeness as God's people, Israel was seen as drawing all nations to itself and to its God so that the original state of community and trust before Adam's fall would be restored.

The great Hebrew prophets dreamed of the day when all nations would stream toward the Lord's house, high up on the mountain of the Lord, in the holy city, Jerusalem. There the nations would beat their spears into pruning hooks and their swords into plowshares. Having put war forever aside, all nations would walk together in the light of the Lord (Isaiah 2:2-5; 66:18-24). Reconciliation and unity would be so total that even Sodom would be included (Ezekiel 16:53). Not only would Israel then live in perfect harmony, but the whole of humankind would be at one and at peace as in the primeval solidarity of creation.

It was a compelling dream, an inviting vision. It foresaw even the total restoration of humanity's bond with the world of nature. There would be a new earth and new heavens. Wolf and lamb, leopard and kid, calf and young lion would graze together. Baby and cobra would play together (Isaiah 11:1-9). Completely at home again in a friendly world, all humanity would come together to praise the one Lord of all, each worshiping in their own language (Isaiah 66:18-24). Total harmony would be restored as in the days before Adam and Eve ruptured their union with God, one another and the rest of creation.

As time went on, the prophets saw this dream of universal solidarity coming to be through the presence of a mysterious representative of God. Ezekiel saw God appointing one shepherd to pasture his torn flock. That shepherd was to be a servant-king in the line of David (Ezekiel 34:21-31). Isaiah had earlier developed extended descriptions of God's "servant"—a "suffering servant"—who would bring unity and peace and be a light for the nations (Isaiah 42:1-9; 52:13-53:12). Later, Daniel ascribed this unifying mission to the "son of man" whose dominion would extend to the four kingdoms of the earth (Daniel 7:13-27).

Familiar with the Scriptures, Jesus seems to have recognized that those dreams of universal harmony were coming true in his own person and ministry. Wherever he went in Galilee, Judea, Samaria and even the region of the Hellenic Ten Cities, Jesus' presence brought people of all persuasions to faith in himself and openness to one another. As he drew people to himself and to one another, Jesus spoke to them about their ancient ideals of unity in a fresh, challenging way. Like a city on a mountaintop, they were to be an attractive light to others (Matthew 5:14-16).

At times, Jesus implied that the ancient images of God's unifying representative were being realized in himself. He suggested that he was the "shepherd" (Mark 14:47), the "son of man," (Matthew 8:20), the "king" (Matthew 25:31-32), the "servant" (Matthew 20:28). In fact, Jesus seems to be the very first person to unite together the two mysterious figures of Isaiah and Daniel—the "servant" and the "son of man." His words and actions suggest that Jesus realized his unique role in bringing about the long dream of harmony between all peoples.

He was also aware that not all viewed him and his ministry in that light. Influential Jewish leaders saw Jesus' efforts to break down barriers as a serious threat to the purity of the Jewish nation. Jesus was aware of their plots to silence him.

It is that awareness that gives special poignancy to the story of what was to be Jesus' "last supper" with his friends. For the Jews of Jesus' time, a meal was a special symbol of unity, of fellowship. Jesus gathered his closest disciples around him at the very time his enemies plotted against him. He broke bread with them and shared with them a common cup. There was a sense of intimate closeness, but a cloud hung over their experience of unity. Jesus expressed his sense of how fragile that unity was in the face of what he knew was coming. As they all left the supper room, Jesus told his friends that they would be scattered when he, their shepherd, would be struck down (Mark 14:27).

When, in fact, Jesus was struck down a few hours later, his friends did indeed scatter into the safety of darkness. Many, like the two setting out for Emmaus, left the community of disciples in disillusionment (Luke 24:13-14). The hoped-for realization of their dream seemed totally thwarted. Their sad journey symbolizes the fragmentation caused by Jesus' death.

The fragmentation and disillusionment were short lived. The surprising experience of the risen Lord drew the frightened disciples back together. The unifying power of the Lord's presence is suggested by the hasty return of the two from Emmaus back to the community in Jerusalem (Luke 24:25-30).

In the ensuing weeks and months, the community of Jesus' followers grew steadily. Their numbers eventually included people from many parts of the world, including non-Jews. The unifying presence of the risen Christ was increasingly felt.

As the communities celebrated the Lord's presence by "breaking bread" together, they reflected with the apostles on the life and teachings of Jesus (Acts 2:42-47). In the process of trying to understand better their own experience of unity in the presence of the risen Lord, they naturally turned to the Hebrew Scriptures. As they did so, the meaning of what Jesus did and said became clearer to them. So they shared with others their new understanding.

They explicitly related Israel's dream of worldwide

unity to Jesus, and saw him as God's agent in making that dream come true. They clearly saw Jesus as the "light of the world" (John 8:12), a light in which all nations would walk together. He was the "good shepherd" forming one flock by drawing all to himself (John 10:1-18). Jesus' unifying, reconciling role as "son of man" and "servant" became a central symbol for interpreting Jesus' ministry, beginning with his baptism by John (Mark 1:9-11).

The Lord's Supper came to be seen clearly as a celebration of unity with the risen Lord and with the community. Jesus at the last supper is recognized as the "servant" (John 13:1-17). His prayer is "that all may be one" (John 17:21). The bread he breaks and calls his body becomes the food of unity, forming those who share the one loaf into one body (1 Corinthians 10:17). That one body is the body of Christ, with the risen Lord as its head (1 Corinthians 12:12-31; Ephesians 4:1-16). Ever since, the Eucharist has been celebrated by Christians as the sacrament of Christ's presence, the deepest source of Christian unity.

The death of Jesus on the cross was eventually seen as the central act of God's plan for universal unity. Jesus died "to gather into one all the dispersed children of God" (John 11:52). Dying, Jesus sends forth into the world his unifying Spirit (John 19:30). Now "the last Adam has become a life-giving Spirit" (1 Corinthians 15:45).

The unifying power of the Spirit is dramatically described as healing the divisions among peoples, divisions that originated at the Tower of Babel (Genesis 11:1-9). For at Pentecost, the Spirit draws together "devout Jews of every nation under heaven," who heard God's good news "each in his own language" (Acts 2:1-12). In this experience of unity in Christ's Spirit, the Church of Christ was born.

Over the years a wealth of images were drawn from the Hebrew Bible to show the unity of the Church with the risen Christ as its center. The Church is God's new "people" united under the leadership of Jesus Christ (1

Corinthians 1:2); it is a "building" whose capstone is Christ Jesus (Ephesians 2:13–22). We form one "flock" led by a single shepherd (John 10:1–16). We are branches of the one "vine," who is Jesus Christ (John 15:1–17). We are heirs with Christ in God's one "family" (Romans 8:14–17). In that family "there does not exist. . .Jew or Greek, slave or freeman, male or female. All are one in Christ Jesus" (Galatians 3:28). That one family of God opens its arms to all the nations of the earth (Acts 15:13–21).

Christian insight into the unifying power of Christ's presence went one step further. The ultimate plan of God, his mystery, goes even beyond the overcoming of alienation between peoples. The ancient Jewish dream saw a unified humanity living in total harmony with the world of nature. For the Christians who created the New Testament, that dream meant that God's plan was "to bring all things in the heavens and on earth into one under Christ's headship" (Ephesians 1:10). Not only is the risen Lord head of a reconciled humanity but he is also what ultimately unites the created universe. Mysteriously he "fills the universe in all its parts" (Ephesians 1:22) and "in him everything continues in being" (Colossians 1:17). Christ's reconciling presence has the power to "reconcile everything in his person, both on earth and in the heavens" (Colossians 1:15–20). In Jesus Christ, the primeval harmony of paradise is restored. In the vision of new heavens and a new earth there will be complete unity, total harmony (Revelation 21:1–21).

Such is the ultimate Christian assessment of Christ's unifying presence. It is a dream whose fulfillment has already begun in the life and teachings of Jesus of Nazareth. It is a dream of unity that finds further realization wherever people are led to break down divisive barriers and accept one another in trust and love. It is a longing of the human heart hinted at by a little black fish who taught his fellow fish to swim together. It is a dream that can come true in Jesus Christ, whom St. Augustine called simply "our unifier."

10

Jesus Christ Challenging Presence

*M*ary sat quietly, self-assuredly. She was telling me about her summer as a volunteer recreation worker. "I never thought I could do something like that," she admitted. "I grew up with everything I wanted. My parents saw that I received a good education. They gave me just about everything most people my age would like to have. But I felt bored. I needed a challenge. Something important seemed to be missing."

I listened without comment. Mary continued. "Then one day I read a story about a statue of Jesus. It was found in a bombed-out church. The hands of the statue had been blown off. An American soldier found the statue in the rubble of the church but he could not find the hands. So he set up the statue and placed a handwritten sign beside it. His sign read, 'Now you must be his hands.' "

I remembered the story. Apparently it happened near the end of World War II, probably in France.

"That really touched me," Mary went on. "I felt a strong desire to do something, to reach out to help others. I sensed a kind of challenge from Christ to do something for him. That same week I saw a notice on the bulletin board at school. Missionaries on a Sioux reservation needed a volunteer recreation director for the summer.

Mary paused for a moment. She smiled and said, "I already had plans for three weeks of the summer. I was going to the beach. But that story of the statue without hands kept haunting me. The notice seemed to show me a way that I could become his hands; it looked like a real challenge. So a few days later, I volunteered. It was a tremendous experience. I hope I helped those young people as much as they helped me."

As Mary described what she did during the summer on the reservation, I was captivated by her joy and enthusiasm. I could not help thinking of another young person faced with a similar challenge. He, too, had just about everything he wanted or needed, but like Mary, felt a desire for something more. My memory of him was such a contrast with Mary. His face was sad, his spirits downcast.

The young man had just met Jesus of Nazareth and had eagerly asked him what more he could do with his life. Jesus liked him and sensed his longing. Jesus invited him to give up his riches, share them with the poor, and become his disciple. The young man felt the challenge. But, even more, he felt the pull of possessions and a comfortable life. He lowered his eyes and looked away from Jesus. Sadly he walked away (Matthew 19:16-23).

Mary's experience and that of the rich young man of the Gospel dramatize a vital dimension of the reality of Jesus. His presence is inevitably a challenging presence. His presence normally leads to a crisis within one, a moment of decision. So it has been from the very start of his public ministry.

Jesus' first recorded words as a wandering rabbi in Galilee were words of exciting challenge. He told everyone who would listen that "this is the time of fulfillment. The reign of God is at hand!" (Mark 1:15). What he meant was that the long-awaited outpouring of God's powerful love was taking place. His words were of unbelievable divine kindness and promise. He assured his listeners that it was really happening before their very eyes. They could be a part of God's gentle but mighty rule of love.

The opportunity was present. The challenge was clear. There would be no force, but an insistent call: "Reform your lives and believe in the gospel!" (Mark 1:15). The

challenge flowed from the attractiveness of God's
unimagined benevolence: "Believe this incredibly good
news and live accordingly."

The life-changing implications of accepting the challenge quickly became clear. Fishermen left nets, boats,
family and everything else to share with Jesus God's
promised reign. Blind and lame who genuinely believed
found new vision and mobility. Prostitutes who accepted
the challenge found themselves truly loved. Greedy tax
collectors like Zacchaeus found unexpected riches in giving back what they had stolen. Wise religious leaders
like Nicodemus discovered still deeper wisdom. Sinners
of all kinds found mercy and forgiveness.

But others found the challenge hard to accept. It
seems that Jesus' relatives and the religious leaders
found greater difficulties than most. His relatives
tended to consider him insane, while those "learned in
the law" found him an agent of Beelzebub, the evil one.

Jesus' teaching was forthright in spelling out the
dimensions of the challenge occasioned by the coming to
be of God's gracious reign. His early preaching is
summed up in the "great discourse" reconstructed in the
Gospels according to Matthew and Luke. Both versions
reveal a challenge that cuts to the heart of every listener.

The love required of those who accept God's reign of
love is to embrace, as does God's love, even enemies,
those who hate you, those who attack you and treat you
badly. The perfection of those who accept God's call to
perfection, is to be as compassionate to all as the Father
of all is compassionate.

Accepting God's good news of grace is not just a matter of repeating, "Lord, Lord!" It involves practicing
what Jesus teaches. It involves doing the will of God. It
is a matter of the heart, of total, single-minded commitment and trust.

Jesus lays down the challenge in graphic terms: If
your eye leads you to sin, gouge it out. Cut off your hand
if it leads you away from God's will. Better to be maimed
than to be damned. (See Matthew 5:29–30).

There are just two roads, one smooth and wide leading
to destruction, the other narrow and rough leading to
life. There are only two kinds of trees—known from their
fruits—sound ones and decaying ones. Those that bear
bad fruit are cut down and burned. There are two possible masters of one's heart. You cannot serve them both
and find God's blessing. There are beatitudes—bless-
ings—for those who choose God's will. For the rest, there
are contrasting woes.

The challenge that Jesus spells out is all-encompass-
ing, demanding. The only acceptable response is total
commitment matched with total trust. Jesus reassures
those who fearfully face so weighty a choice: Their
Father in heaven knows all their needs, and cares for
them more than he cares for the rest of the world. So
trust him completely.

Jesus' parables during the rest of his ministry place
before his hearers the attractiveness of God's reign and
the totality of its claim. The price is high, but the reward
far outstrips any cost. It makes obvious sense to sell all
you own in order to buy a field in which a treasure lies
hidden, a treasure worth considerably more than all one
now possesses. A merchant who finds one pearl more
precious than all the rest he already has, does the right
thing to sell them all in order to buy the one really
precious pearl.

Jesus never attempts to gloss over the high cost of
discipleship in God's kingdom. Commitment to God will
take precedence over every other affection, even the love
of parents. It means taking up one's cross daily. It
means being willing to lose one's life in the hope of gain-
ing fuller life. There is no valid excuse accepted for not
coming to the banquet of the king. You need to become
like a child once again, full of total trust in the Father,
placing yourself completely in his hands.

Such is the challenge Jesus preached as he announced
the coming of God's mighty love. Jesus calls his hearers
to a total reorientation of life, the complete surrender of
self to God's will. Acceptance of God's will involves a

decisive change of heart, an undivided heart, a single-minded spirit. The supreme norm of life now becomes the will of the Father. And the broad lines of that will are clear: love and trust God by acting as he does, with un-conditional compassion and care for every human being.

What Jesus asked of others, he lived himself. The Gospels record his single-minded pursuit of the Father's will. Leaving home, he placed the Father's will above even the closest of family ties. One day, when his dis-ciples told him that his mother and other close relatives were at the door, he told those who were listening to him, "Whoever does the will of God is brother and sister and mother to me" (Mark 3:35).

Jesus' commitment to the Father's will for him was one of unswerving fidelity, but one that cost continual struggle. Throughout Jesus' ministry, he was faced by a recurring and attractive temptation. It was the funda-mental temptation we all face: between self-seeking and seeking God's will. For him, the temptation took on a unique form, centering on his leadership role in the com-ing reign of God. In its simplest form, the temptation was between accepting the popular view of the Messiah —a revolutionary who would lead the people against the Roman legions, driving them out of Israel, and then be-come the king of a liberated nation—and God's view of the Messiah. As the days went on, it became clearer to Jesus that God's view was one of compassionate service, culmin-ating in rejection and suffering, perhaps even in death.

The temptation is summarized in the Gospels as a dramatic confrontation between Jesus and Satan in the desert. The struggle hinges on the nature of power to which Jesus is drawn: the power of popularity and force, or the power of obedient service. Jesus, turning to the Scriptures to refute Satan, chooses a leadership of trust and love rather than of self-glorification and power. Such is God's will as he perceives it.

Later in Jesus' ministry, the temptation recurs in a particularly poignant manner. After months of immense popularity, Jesus finds that fewer and fewer people take his challenge seriously. The influential religious leaders were the first to turn away from him and his message. Gradually the crowds became smaller and smaller. Soon only a relatively small group of people, generally considered the most insignificant, came out to hear him. In what must have been a moment of deep discouragement, Jesus reveals the totality of his response to God, his Father. He prays, "Father, it is true. You have graciously willed it so" (Matthew 11:26).

That same single-minded acceptance of the Father's will led Jesus to preach with even greater urgency the message of compassion despite the growing hostility against him. As the outcome becomes more evident to Jesus and more imminent, he becomes beset with fear. Confiding his anguish and sadness to his closest friends, he withdraws to pray alone. Weakened by utter terror before the horror he knew awaited him, Jesus pleaded with the Father to allow him another way. Yet over and over he prayed: "Father, let it be as you would have it, not as I. . .your will be done" (Matthew 26:39–42).

The same total surrender to the Father's will finds expression in the midst of the mental and physical agony of crucifixion. Jesus died as he had lived, seeking only his Father's will. With his final breath, even though feeling abandoned even by God, he surrenders his life into the hands of the Father: "Father, into your hands I commend my spirit" (Luke 23:46). Even in the moment of greatest agony, his compassion and mercy find expression in a plea for forgiveness of the very persons who have brought him to such an awful end: "Father, forgive them; they do not know what they are doing" (Luke 23:34).

That moment of Jesus' death on the cross presented his friends and disciples with the greatest challenge of their lives. Jesus lived according to his perception of God's will just as he taught them to do, but where had it led him? Was this the outcome of accepting God's rule? Was this the gracious reign of a Father? In final disillusionment, many followers turned away for other more promising challenges. Many were now convinced that

Jesus was indeed a false prophet. A faithful few continued to accept Jesus' vision and challenge, but the evidence of his violent death profoundly troubled them. To those closest to him, his death posed a greater challenge to faith and love than did his life.

Then, to their amazement, his faithful friends experienced him again alive. His presence was reassuring and a source of unbounded joy. But the presence of the risen Christ brought a renewed sense of challenge. Some, like Thomas, had serious doubts and hesitation. Peter had his own anxieties, after betraying Jesus. No doubt each of the others had their secret fears. But all was overcome by the presence of their risen Lord. They accepted his command to go out and proclaim the good news to the whole of creation. He promised to be with them until the end of time.

As they carried out his mission in the changing circumstances of their lives, Jesus' disciples were driven by their heartfelt affection for and admiration of the risen Christ. "The love of Christ impels us," wrote Paul (2 Corinthians 5:14). That was the way they now perceived the challenge of the kingdom. Love was focused on Jesus Christ, who came to be recognized as embodying in his own person the ultimate norm of action. The basic choice or challenge centered on him: do you love him and accept him as your Lord, or not? Jesus himself was now seen as the law, the model. The concrete way of discovering God's will in one's life was to be the way of imitating Jesus Christ. The fundamental challenge facing Christians was to live in their own circumstances and unique situations the way Jesus lived, and to do so in union with him whose presence remained an insistent challenge.

"Your attitude must be that of Christ," urged Paul in writing to the Christian community at Philippi (Philippians 2:5). "Put on the Lord Jesus Christ," he writes the Roman Christians (Romans 13:14). Putting on Christ involved reproducing in one's own life the motivation and manner of acting that governed the life of Jesus himself. The early Christians recalled stories of Jesus' life and examples of his teaching. His words and acts became normative. They remembered how he lived and they tried to live in that same spirit within their quite different circumstances.

The imitation was grounded in inner configuration of spirit between Jesus and his followers. Imitating Christ was less a detailed imitation of his mannerisms than an identification with his spirit. "Continue therefore to live in Christ Jesus the Lord, in the spirit in which you received him. Be rooted in him and built up in him, growing ever stronger in faith, as you were taught, and overflowing with gratitude" (Colossians 2:6-7).

Ultimately the challenge facing the Christian is, with the help of Christ's Spirit, to live as Jesus lived. "It is a life of faith in the Son of God, who loved me and gave himself up for me" (Galatians 2:19-20). In its most succinct form the challenge is to "love one another as I have loved you" (John 15:12).

Surprising as it may seem, that awesome challenge brings peace, joy, fulfillment. Mary experienced some of that in accepting the challenge to reach out as Jesus' hands to the needy on the Sioux reservation. She responded to the challenging presence of Jesus Christ, with us always and everywhere.

Epilogue

What was Jesus really like? What difference does Jesus Christ make? These were the questions with which we began. They led inevitably to a third question. Where can we meet Jesus Christ today?

In our search we discovered much about what Jesus of Nazareth was really like. We found him to be a fascinating, mysterious personality. He suffered like us, died as we must, was tempted as we all are. His contemporaries saw him as a prophet like the great Hebrew prophets of Israel. He preached with unusual authority, daring to change the law while calling people to observe it. One message seemed to consume him: the imminent coming of God's reign or kingdom.

People saw him as a rabbi, a teacher. They wondered at his wisdom, his great good sense, his insight into life and the Hebrew Scriptures. Yet they puzzled over his lack of rabbinic training and credentials. Those who heard him teach were attracted by his message of mercy, challenged by his call for unconditional love of God and neighbor—even enemies—and captivated by his stories that touched their hearts and minds. As a wandering storyteller he held them spellbound. He evidently had great gifts of imagination as well as a piercing intellect.

The crowds were awed at the amazing deeds of this wonder worker who walked among them. He seemed filled with the power of God, overcoming the most fearful evils of body and spirit and nature. Yet children felt comfortable in his arms, the weak and sinful found strength in his gentleness and tenderness. He seemed at once strangely different, yet intimately close. People stirred to his words of freedom; but they were taken

aback at the very time they were attracted by his surprisingly free lifestyle. The oppressed, the poor, those
dealt with unfairly—all looked to him for liberation.
Some saw him as the long-promised Messiah, but he
seemed to evade being so named.

Despite his popularity and ease with people, Jesus
slipped off frequently to the desert, to the mountains, to
secluded gardens for quiet moments—even entire days
and nights—of prayer. He was clearly a man of God. But
his intimacy with his Father did not hinder his closeness
to people, especially to anyone who was hurting. He was
a supremely sensitive, caring, compassionate man, with
a great capacity for friendship. He seemed most at home
with those on the fringes of proper society. Sinners,
lepers, the handicapped, and the despised were his com-
panions at table.

Yet Jesus was at home as well with the rich and powerful, the learned and religious. He identified himself with
no party. He was neither priest nor Scribe, Pharisee nor
Sadducee, monk nor revolutionary Zealot. Jesus was
open to all, even the despised Samaritans and hated
Romans. He had no time for prejudice of any kind.

Everywhere he went he attracted people by the charm
of his personality and the wisdom of his preaching. He
challenged and invited people, but never forced them. He
called forth the best in people, often a goodness not
suspected before they met him. He drew to himself
disciples who learned to live as he lived. He called all to
accept him, and in accepting him to accept also the
demanding but freeing reign of his Father.

Most of all, in the course of these pages, we glimpsed
his inner spirit. Jesus' drive welled up from commitment
to his Father's will. That will, for him, had to do with the
happiness, the wholeness, the salvation of all people. So
his entire life was given to serving the needs of others.
He surrendered his life into the hands of his Father as he
went about bringing to friend and foe alike the incredible
message of a God who cares.

Jesus' dedicated and loving service for all met with an increasingly cool response after the first months of excited popularity. As the leaders and then the crowds drifted away or turned against him, Jesus sensed that his service of love would be filled with increasing suffering. He seemed to see himself as the mysterious "Son of Man" envisioned by the prophet Daniel, and at the same time the tragic "Suffering Servant" foreseen by Isaiah the prophet. Jesus seems to have seen that somehow the growing conflict would demand the total gift of himself for his fellow humans. He seems to have known that his self-giving would have a decisive impact on humankind. Abandoned and alone, he surrendered his life to his Father for the forgiveness and love of all.

So he appears, this remarkable man of Nazareth. Condemned as a blasphemer by the religious leaders of his people, he was executed by the Romans as a revolutionary. Even his closest friends found themselves turning away in disillusionment. All the dreams and hopes that this mysterious man had stirred in their hearts shattered on the harsh reality of the cross. Only when they met him again, on that great first day of the week, did they begin to glimpse the fullness of his identity and mission.

Drawing on the riches of their Hebrew Scriptures, the disciples of the risen Christ gradually grasped that this man they loved was more than just a great and good man. They began to call Jesus by names previously reserved only to the one God, Yahweh, the God of Abraham, Isaac, and Jacob. "Jesus is Lord" became their creed. In their efforts to express the wonder of who Christ Jesus was to them, they gave him a brilliant array of titles, all of which took on connotations of divinity: Son of God, Word, Light of the World, Way, Wisdom, Savior, Redeemer, Priest, High Priest, Mediator, Son of Man, King, Lord, Servant, Shepherd, Lamb of God.

So our search for the "Jesus of history" has led to the discovery of the "Christ of faith," the God-man; his life, death, and resurrection unlocks the mystery of life and opens human experience to the healing, ennobling presence of the living God. Jesus Christ is seen as both God and man, the savior of humankind. "Jesus Christ, Son of God, Savior," in the Christian shorthand of the ancient fish symbol (icthus).

Our search followed the same development as did the disciples' discovery of who Jesus was and what his task was. Our search began "from below," from human experiences of this compelling man. It led upwards to the very point of departure of the classical christologies of creed and catechism, namely, the divinity of Christ. Creed and catechism begin "from above," from God who became human. Though these starting points seem at opposite ends of the spectrum, both classical and contemporary christologies agree on the essentials of traditional Christian faith in Jesus Christ.

What is perhaps most important for each of us in living that ancient yet ever modern faith in Christ Jesus is the realization that he is risen and with us. Our faith is not one of mere memories. Rather, the memories help us recognize and celebrate the very presence of the risen Christ. Catholic spirituality is a vital openness to the presence of Christ wherever he reveals himself. "Where can we meet Christ today?" is ultimately the perennial question of the Catholic Christian.

Our tradition gives us some answers that have grown out of centuries of Christian experience of the risen Lord's healing, saving presence in daily life. The simplest answer to "Where is he?" is that given by the risen Lord himself as he takes leave of his disciples: "I am with you always, until the end of the world" (Matthew 28:20).

"Always" implies "everywhere." Within the development of the New Testament itself, Christian faith grew to the point of recognizing a "cosmic" presence of Christ. John identifies Christ Jesus as the creative Word of God whose sustaining presence gives life and light to whatever exists (John 1:1-18). Paul affirms that in Christ "everything continues in being" (Colossians 1:17) and proclaims that the risen Lord "fills the universe in all its parts" (Ephesians 1:22).

Subsequent Christian tradition built on this profound New Testament awareness of the presence of Christ that embraces the entire universe. Everything in our world of experience can be seen as a sacrament or sign of Christ's presence. Christian spirituality reduced that insight of faith into a principle of Christian living.

In the 2nd century, St. Irenaeus saw all of reality "recapitulated" in Christ. Two centuries later St. Augustine wrote simply, "History is pregnant with Christ." Much later St. Ignatius Loyola taught his followers in the 16th century to seek Christ in all things. Teilhard de Chardin summed up in modern scientific language the centuries-old sensitivity to the "cosmic" Christ present in the whole of created reality. The world is a visible, tangible sacrament of the presence of the risen Lord.

Of all things that exist, some more clearly reveal Christ's presence than do others. People are the most important signs of the Lord's presence. According to Matthew's Gospel, Jesus mysteriously identifies himself with all human beings, particularly those who suffer. What we do to people, Jesus insists, we do to him (Matthew 25:31-46).

Christian spirituality from New Testament times to our own day has acknowledged the presence of Christ in every human person. The ancient monastic saying sums it all up in a spirit of open hospitality: "When a stranger comes, Christ comes." Stories of great Christian saints translate this faith-conviction into moving examples. An example is the story of Martin of Tours who cut his warm soldier's coat in two and gave half to a shivering beggar, only to discover afterwards that the beggar was Jesus Christ. Countless Christians have learned from an early age to "see Christ in everyone." Each individual is a living sacrament of the presence of Jesus Christ.

Among all the men and women of the world, one group

is called to stand out as a convincing sign of Christ's presence among us, the Church of Jesus Christ. Those who gather together in shared faith in the risen Lord are his "Body." The community of believers is a special sacrament of Christ. St. Paul learned this on the road to Damascus as he went in search of Christians to arrest and persecute. Struck from his horse, he heard the Lord's voice: "I am Jesus, the one you are persecuting" (Acts 9:5). St. Augustine translated Paul's insight into greater detail. Augustine wrote that when someone is baptized, it is Christ himself who baptizes. So it is that the risen Christ is present in his Church to teach, heal, forgive, anoint, lead, and serve. The Church is Jesus Christ extended in time and place.

Within the Church, one particular moment becomes the most striking sacrament of Christ's presences. The eucharistic meal brings into sharpest focus the presence of the Lord of life. In a meal of fellowship on the night before he died, Jesus identified bread and wine with himself. The Gospels recount that Jesus, risen and again with his disciples, shares himself with them—his body and blood—"in the breaking of bread" (Luke 24:30-35). There is also the beautiful story of Jesus sharing a seashore breakfast of bread and fish with his weary disciples shortly after his resurrection—a marvelous picture of the eucharistic presence of Christ with his friends (John 21:9-14).

Where can we meet Christ today? Christians of all ages direct us to search for him in the whole of created reality. To search for him in things, events, and most of all in people. To search for him particularly in our brother and sister Christians, especially as we gather at the eucharistic meal to celebrate his presence with us always and everywhere.

We can learn to experience in those places the presence of the risen Lord. He is with us to embrace us, to enrich our lives, to help us find life's meaning and purpose, to guide us in our search for a better way to live, to strengthen us, free us, pray in and for us, plead for our help, unite us, and challenge us. The heart of our experience is the present reality of Jesus Christ.

Perhaps an ancient prayer, attributed to St. Patrick, and written in the 5th century, best expresses the traditional spirituality rooted in the presence of Christ. It is frequently called "St. Patrick's Breastplate."

> Christ with me, Christ before me, Christ behind me
> Christ in me, Christ beneath me, Christ above me
> Christ on my right, Christ on my left
> Christ when I lie down, Christ when I sit down,
> Christ when I arise
> Christ in the heart of everyone who thinks of me
> Christ in the mouth of everyone who speaks of me
> Christ in every eye that sees me
> Christ in every ear that hears me.

Recommended Books About Jesus

Aron, Robert. *The Jewish Jesus*. Maryknoll, N.Y.: Orbis Books, 1971.
An exploration of the Jewish background of Jesus as it affected his life and ministry.

Boff, Leonardo. *Jesus Christ Liberator*. Maryknoll, N.Y.: Orbis Books, 1978.
A moving, distinctively Latin American interpretation of Jesus' meaning as liberator in today's world.

Buechner, Frederick and Lee Boltin. *The Faces of Jesus*. New York: Simon & Shuster, 1974. (also published under the title, *The Life of Jesus*).
A beautiful book of artists' works showing the many facets of Jesus' life and personality.

Cassidy, Richard J. *Jesus, Politics, and Society*. Maryknoll, N.Y.: Orbis Books, 1978.
An analysis of the social and political conditions of Jesus' times and Luke's report of Jesus' own stance.

Comblin, Jose. *Jesus of Nazareth: Meditations on His Humanity*. Maryknoll, N.Y.: Orbis Books, 1978.
A portrait of Jesus as his disciples knew him before his resurrection.

Donders, Joseph G. *Jesus, the Stranger*. Maryknoll, N.Y.: Orbis Books, 1978.
A series of profoundly simple sermons drawn out of a Dutch priest's long experience in Africa.

Dwyer, John C. *Son of Man and Son of God: A New Language for Faith*. Ramsey, N.J.: Paulist Press, 1983.

A careful coming to terms with the meaning of the documents of the early Christological Councils.

Endo, Shusaku. *A Life of Jesus.* Ramsey, N.J.: Paulist Press, 1978.
A sensitive, compassionate portrait of Jesus through Japanese eyes.

Fitzmyer, Joseph A., S.J. *A Christological Catechism: New Testament Answers.* Ramsey, N.J.: Paulist Press, 1982.
Twenty basic questions about Jesus with answers based on modern biblical studies of the New Testament.

Gray, Donald P. *Jesus: The Way to Freedom.* Winona, Minn: St. Mary's College Press, 1979.
A small, attractively illustrated interpretation of Jesus' freeing presence and power.

Greeley, Andrew M. *The Jesus Myth.* Garden City, N.Y.: Doubleday, 1973.
A clear, moving interpretation of Jesus' life and teachings in the light of recent biblical studies.

Hellwig, Monika K. *Jesus: The Compassion of God.* Wilmington, Del.: Michael Glazier, 1983.
A reinterpretation of traditional understandings of Jesus, rooted in the anguish of people in today's world.

Kappen, Sebastian. *Jesus and Freedom.* Maryknoll, N.Y.: Orbis Books, 1978.
A compelling portrait of Jesus as liberator drawn from an Indian theologian's experience of conditions in India.

Kasper, Walter. *Jesus the Christ.* Ramsey, N.J.: Paulist Press, 1976.
A survey and synthesis of biblical and traditional insights into Jesus in the light of modern philosophy.

Kealy, John P., C.S.Sp. *Who Is Jesus of Nazareth?* Denville, N.J.: Dimension Books, 1977.
A portrait of Jesus drawn from Mark's Gospel in the light of modern scholarship.

Kung, Hans. *On Being a Christian*. Garden City, N.Y.: Doubleday, 1976.
A reinterpretation of traditional understandings of Jesus in the light of contemporary thought.

Lane, Dermot A. *The Reality of Jesus*. Ramsey, N.J.: Paulist Press, 1975.
A concise, readable, up-to-date presentation of contemporary Christology.

Mackey, James P. *Jesus the Man and the Myth*. Ramsey, N.J.: Paulist Press, 1979.
An effort to detect the historical Jesus behind the development of the Christian tradition about Jesus.

McCauley, Michael F. *The Jesus Book*. Chicago: Thomas More Press, 1978.
A kaleidoscope of images of and words about Jesus by artists and writers down through the ages.

Nolan, Albert. *Jesus Before Christianity*. Maryknoll, N.Y.: Orbis Books, 1978.
A book from the South African experience of the life of Jesus as a practical response to worldwide suffering.

O'Collins, Gerald, S.J. *What are they saying about Jesus?* Ramsey, N.J.: Paulist Press, 1977.
A very small book that pulls together and summarizes contemporary theological trends regarding Jesus.

———. *Interpreting Jesus*. Ramsey, N.J.: Paulist Press, 1983.
A contemporary construction of a Christology drawing on the best biblical scholarship.

O'Grady, John F. *Jesus, Lord and Christ*. Ramsey, N.J.: Paulist Press, 1973.
A very readable interpretation of Jesus arranged according to the biblical titles given to Jesus.

Schillebeeckx, Edward. *Jesus*. New York: Seabury Press, 1979.
———. *Christ*. New York: Seabury Press, 1980.
A masterful review and creative interpretation of recent scholarship about Jesus who became the Christ.

Senior, Donald. *Jesus: A Gospel Portrait*. Dayton, Ohio: Pflaum Press, 1975.
A readable presentation of those aspects of Jesus' life and teachings on which there is broad scholarly agreement.

Shea, John. *The Challenge of Jesus*. Garden City, N.Y.: Doubleday, 1977.
A popular, readable study of Jesus' life and importance grounded in sound biblical scholarship.

Sloyan, Gerard S. *Jesus in Focus: A Life in Its Setting*. Mystic, Conn.: Twenty-Third Publications, 1983.
A sensitive probing behind what people believed about Jesus, a well informed introductory study of Jesus' teachings and career.

Sobrino, Jon, S.J. *Christology at the Crossroads*. Maryknoll, N.Y.: Orbis Books, 1978.
A profound, provocative book about Jesus and his impact from a Latin American liberation theology perspective.

Wahlberg, Rachel Conrad. *Jesus According to a Woman*. Ramsey, N.J.: Paulist Press, 1975.
A unique approach to understanding Jesus through the perspective of a woman.